The Girl's Guide to Building a Fort

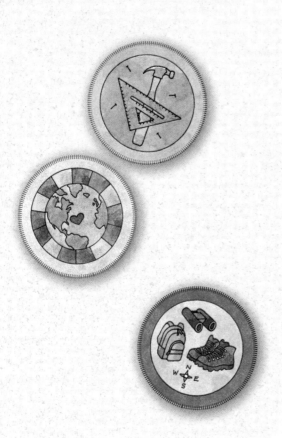

the GiRL'S Guide to BuiLding a FORt

OUTDOOR + INDOOR ADVENTURES FOR HANDS-ON GIRLS

JENNY FIERI

ILLUSTRATIONS BY ALEXIS SEABROOK

Andrews McMeel
PUBLISHING®

Andrews McMeel Publishing
a division of Andrews McMeel Universal
1130 Walnut Street, Kansas City, Missouri 64106

www.andrewsmcmeel.com

Readers are urged to take all appropriate precautions before undertaking
any how-to task. Always read and follow instructions and safety warnings for
all tools and materials, and call in a professional if the task stretches your
abilities too far. Although every effort has been made to provide the best
possible information in this book, neither the publisher nor the author are
responsible for accidents, injuries, or damage incurred as a result of tasks
undertaken by readers. This book is not a substitute for professional services.

Always follow safety and commonsense cooking protocol while
using kitchen utensils, operating ovens and stoves, and handling
uncooked food. If children are assisting in the preparation of
any recipe, they should always be supervised by an adult.

21 22 23 24 25 SDB 10 9 8 7 6 5 4 3 2 1

ISBN: 978-1-5248-6117-9

Library of Congress Control Number: 2020945525

Editor: Allison Adler
Art Director: Diane Marsh
Production Editor: Elizabeth A. Garcia
Production Manager: Chuck Harper

Made by:
King Yip (Dongguan) Printing & Packaging Factory Ltd.
Address and location of manufacturer:
Daning Administrative District, Humen Town
Dongguan Guangdong, China 523930
1st Printing—1/25/21

Contents

LET'S BE CHEFS! 157

YOU ROCKED IT!: BADGES FOR HANDS-ON GIRLS 204

TO THE LITTLE GIRL INSIDE US ALL WHO
WANTS TO COME OUT AND PLAY

INTRODUCTION

Welcome to the wild and adventurous world of hands-on girls! What's a hands-on girl? Hands-on girls fix things; we make things; we experiment; we play; and we end each day tired and happy and probably a little dirty. We know how to hammer a nail, and we can tell you all about the stars and their names. We know which plants to avoid in the woods and which plants to grow in the garden. We race outside the minute we can for a quick hike or a game, and we spend rainy days building forts or test-flying paper airplanes.

Maybe you do none of those things right now, or maybe you do just a few of them. That's OK! The most important thing about being a hands-on girl is that we love to try new things. We'll try on this, we'll test out that, we'll play a new role for a day or an afternoon. That's what this book is really about. It's about exploring and learning to listen to the voice inside of you that tells you what you really like. In these pages, you'll get to try on a bunch of hats—scientist, trailblazer, athlete, artist, builder, and chef—without having to sign up for a class or a team, buy a bunch of new equipment, or lose all your after-school free time.

With this book, you can test out what it's like to be an astronomer who can name the stars, or an ornithologist who can lead a bird-watching expedition, or a scientist who can experiment with chemical reactions in a lab, all in the first chapter. In Chapter 2, we'll hit the trail, just like the naturalists, pioneers, and other trailblazing women who explored the American frontier before us. You'll learn survival skills like how to build a fire, how to get unlost in the woods, and how to tie the five most useful knots. You'll also learn how to plan mindful nature walks, how to perfectly stock a campsite, and how to make the best s'mores of your life along the way.

In Chapter 3, we'll lace up our sneakers for some super-fun games—giving the classics you know, like softball, hopscotch, and jump rope, fun new twists to make them more challenging and more exciting for hands-on girls like you. And for those days when we can't run around outside, you can find card games for smarties and simple self-defense moves that will help you karate chop away an otherwise boring afternoon.

If you like art, or you're not sure what kind of art you like, try some watercolor painting, splatter painting, hand-lettering, or nature photography activities found in Chapter 4. Or kick back with a book in a new-to-you genre from The Hands-On Girl's Reading List, found on page 124. Or maybe you'd like to try woodworking and building things? The only way to find out is to tackle some of the activities in Chapter 5, where you'll find step-by-step instructions to build, sand, and paint your own tree swing, fort, bench, and race car, all of which you could do in just a few hours after school.

And if your artistic impulses lean more toward the culinary arts, then we have a whole chapter of fun food challenges, pro-level tips, and recipes for you. You'll get to see what it's like to grow your own herb and vegetable garden, make your own jerky and dried fruit, and up your chopping game with a knife skills tutorial, all of which is way easier than you'd think.

Anytime you complete five activities from a chapter, you'll earn a Hands-On Girl Badge, which you can find at the back of this book. You can also rack up bonus badges, like the Jane-of-All-Trades Badge, which you can earn by completing one activity from each chapter, or the Outdoorsy or Indoorsy Badges, which are awarded for trying six outdoor or six indoor activities. And because hands-on girls are always looking for ways to watch out for others, you can also earn the Good Friend, Good Neighbor, and Good Citizen Badges for acts of kindness to a friend, a neighbor, or the planet.

Whatever you try in this book, never be afraid to be honest about whether you like it or not. Maybe softball is totally not your thing, but you could spend all day chopping veggies in the kitchen. Maybe you're happiest when you're reading on the couch or walking through the park instead of working in the woodshop. Whatever it is, it's never wrong and it's always right, because it's right for you.

Because at the core of every hands-on girl, there's a burning flame of You—what you like and what you don't like, what makes you special and unique—that this book hopes to throw some kindling on. Think of these activities as fuel for figuring out and nurturing your passions and interests. Some pieces will take; some will sputter. But all will teach you a little bit more about which way to go next. And wherever that takes you, you can have the wildest, most amazingly fun time getting there if you kick back and enjoy the ride.

So grab your sneakers, apron, lab coat, or whatever else you need, scan through the Table of Contents on the previous pages to see what sounds the most fun to you, and let's go get hands-on!

CHAPTER 1:

Let's Be Scientists!

Scientists are smart, creative, and always curious, which is why hands-on girls make such great ones. Most scientists start out by making a hypothesis about what's happening in the world around them—an educated guess about anything from "Why is the sky blue?" to "What happens when I mix this with that?" Then they find a way to test their hypothesis, and—BOOM!—just like that, a new scientific discovery is made. So snap on your goggles, step into the laboratory, and let's get our science on.

THE HANDS-ON GIRL'S LAB

Science can be complex, but in many ways it's also very simple. The surprising thing about science is that you don't need tons of complicated equipment or a shiny, sterile lab to start making discoveries. In fact, you can find household versions of the most common scientific equipment in your own kitchen. So set up your simplified lab, or get as sophisticated as you want—either way, get ready to be dazzled by the scientific wonders of the world around us.

THE SIMPLIFIED LAB

Want to experiment with experimentation? Collect these supplies from around the house, and you'll find that you have nearly everything you need to tackle the experiments in this book and get scientific in a snap!

- [ ] **Clear plastic cups**
- [ ] **Scissors**
- [ ] **Kitchen timer or sand timer**
- [ ] **Pencil or colored pencils**
- [ ] **Notebook**
- [ ] **Measuring spoons and cups**
- [ ] **Food coloring**
- [ ] **Ruler**
- [ ] **Binoculars**

THE SOPHISTICATED LAB

Ready to go deeper with your experiments? With a few additional supplies, you'll be ready to conduct hundreds of more sophisticated science experiments.

- ☐ **Plastic beakers with graduations**
- ☐ **Plastic test tubes**
- ☐ **Plastic pipettes or droppers**
- ☐ **Plastic tweezers**
- ☐ **Magnifying glass**
- ☐ **Funnel**
- ☐ **Rubber or latex gloves**
- ☐ **Goggles**
- ☐ **Lab coat**

CLOUDS AND THEIR NAMES

Quick! Picture a cloud. Can you describe what it looks like? Is it white and fluffy, or gray and thin, or maybe it even has a rainbow arcing out of it? Whatever type of cloud floated across your mind, it has a scientific name. In meteorology, which is the science of weather, every cloud has a category that describes its shape and its place in the sky. Here are the three main types of clouds:

CIRRUS CLOUDS are high up in the air and wispy. They look light and feathery because they're made of thin layers of ice crystals. These clouds are so thin that they're transparent and they can appear red and yellow at sunrise and sunset.

STRATUS CLOUDS also form in long, horizontal layers, but they can cover the whole sky and float much lower than cirrus clouds. These clouds can float so low that they can become ground fog or mist. That means that whenever you enter a foggy area, you're actually standing inside a giant cloud!

CUMULUS CLOUDS look like mounds of cotton balls and are one of the most easily recognizable types of cloud. The word "cumulus" comes from the Latin word for "pile." These clouds collect at low levels and are usually scattered across the sky. If they're white, then the weather will be beautiful, but if they're gray, then it might be raining underneath that cloud.

Now that you know the three main types of clouds and their names, take some friends cloud watching and show off your knowledge by naming as many clouds as possible!

THE STARS AND THEIR NAMES

Do you know what the brightest star in the sky is? Here's a hint: you can't see it at night.

That's right—the brightest star is the sun! It's what our whole world literally revolves around, and we'd be totally lost without it.

You might not know as much about the next-brightest star, the North Star. The North Star, also called Polaris, is easy to find with the help of the Big Dipper. The Big Dipper is a constellation, which is a group of stars that are named after what ancient stargazers thought they looked like. It's maybe the most important star group in our sky because of its size, interesting shape, and the fact that it never sets in the sky over North America. It's called the Dipper because it's shaped like a big ladle, with a long, bent handle. Two of its stars, sometimes called the Pointers, always guide you to the North Star.

The North Star is really the most important of the stars in our sky because it marks the direction of north at all times. All the other stars seem to swing around it once every twenty-four hours. But even though it's the most important star, the North Star is actually not a very bright star. It would be super hard to spot except for the help of the Pointers of the Big Dipper. Old-fashioned names for the North Star are the "Home Star" and "The Star That Never Moves."

The coolest part of the Big Dipper is that you can use it to tell time. Just imagine the North Star as the center of a clock and the handle of the Big Dipper as the hour hand. The Big Dipper goes once around the North Star about every twenty-four hours. If the handle of the Big Dipper is about a quarter of the way around the North Star, that would mean about a quarter of a day, or six hours, had passed.

Even though there are trillions of stars in the universe, there are only about five thousand we can see without a telescope. And only twenty of those are stars of the first magnitude, meaning they're the brightest. Have you heard of any of these brightest-of-the-bright stars and the constellations they're part of?

THE FIRST TWENTY STARS IN ORDER OF BRIGHTNESS

1. Sirius, the Dog Star
2. Canopus, of the Ship
3. Rigil Kentaurus, of the Centaur
4. Arcturus, of the Herdsman
5. Vega, of the Lyre
6. Capella, of the Charioteer
7. Rigel, of Orion
8. Procyon, the Little Dog Star
9. Achernar, of Eridanus
10. Betelgeuse, of Orion
11. Hadar, of the Centaur
12. Acrux, of the Southern Cross
13. Altair, of the Eagle
14. Aldebaran, of the Bull
15. Antares, of the Scorpion
16. Spica, of the Virgin
17. Pollux, of the Twins
18. Fomalhaut, of the Southern Fish
19. Becrux, of the Southern Cross
20. Deneb, of the Swan

HOW WIND WORKS

Wind is one of the most powerful forces on earth—it can power giant cities, push huge sailboats, and knock down entire neighborhoods. Wind is air that moves horizontally, and it can be gentle like a cool summer's breeze or fierce like gusts from a tornado that can lift cows right off the ground (imagine lifting a cow!). But what makes wind powerful or weak? Hint: Think about temperature.

Wind is created when air moves from a high-pressure area to a low-pressure area, and the pressure is controlled by an area's temperature. If the difference between the high and low pressures is greater, then the wind is stronger. If the difference is smaller, then the wind is weaker.

If you want to tell the exact direction the wind is blowing, dip your finger in water and put it high in the air. Now you can feel which way the wind is going! The direction of wind is influenced by three things: pressure gradient force, Coriolis force, and friction. The pressure gradient force makes air move from high to low areas of pressure. The Coriolis force makes things in the Northern Hemisphere turn toward the right and things in the Southern Hemisphere turn toward the left. It's caused by the rotation of the earth. And finally, friction changes how the wind flows over the earth's rough and bumpy surface.

Scientists and engineers can use all of this information to make renewable energy from the wind. They build giant wind turbines that have angled blades and spin when they catch the wind. These turbines move and look a lot like pinwheels but on a massive scale. Pinwheels won't power a city, but they will show you when the wind is blowing and how fast it's moving.

RAINY DAY ACTIVITY

MAKE YOUR OWN MINI WIND TURBINE

MATERIALS

- **Sheet of 8.5 by 11-inch paper**
- **Scissors**
- **Ruler**
- **Pencil**

- **Markers or colored pencils for decorating (optional)**
- **Pin (like a long pushpin or thumbtack)**
- **Thin dowel rod**

INSTRUCTIONS

1. Cut your paper into a square.

2. Using a ruler, draw a diagonal line from the top right corner to the bottom left corner and draw another line from the top left corner to the bottom right corner. If you want to decorate your wind turbine, now is a great time to do that!

3. Make a pencil mark on each line about one-third of the way from the center of the paper.

4. Cut along each line and stop cutting at your pencil marks.

5. Bend every other point into the center and push the pin through the four points. The pin should poke all the way through the pinwheel's back.

6. Gently move the pin around to make the pinhole a little larger. This lets the turbine spin.

7. Pin your turbine to your dowel rod—now your wind turbine is ready to catch some air! See how fast you can make it spin, and then try leaving it outside to watch how strong the wind is blowing!

THE TEN BIRDS YOU NEED TO KNOW

Did you know that there are about ten thousand different species of birds worldwide? Birds come in all shapes—like curvy, pink flamingos and squat penguins—and in all sizes—like ostriches, which can grow up to six feet tall. You can spot them anywhere: in cities, forests, deserts, and your own backyard! With so many birds in the world, it's impossible to find and learn about each one, but if you're ready to take on the challenge of boosting your birding knowledge, here are the ten most common birds you might spot. Check these birds off your list when you find them!

1. AMERICAN CROW

Do you have a dog or cat? Well, the American crow might be smarter than them. This large, all-black bird is known for screaming "*caw!*" and for inventing clever tricks to get food. These supersmart problem solvers like visiting yards with bird feeders and using tools to get as much birdseed as possible. Crows sometimes hang out together in huge flocks (sometimes called "murders"), especially in the winter.

2. AMERICAN GOLDFINCH

The American goldfinch is a little yellow bird. A male finch has a black patch on its head that looks like a hat, while females are hatless and a duller shade of yellow. This bird is so light that they can perch on flowers to pull out fluff for their nests and seeds for their dinner. Because goldfinches are small and quick, you'll have to keep your eyes peeled for yellow flashes next time you're on a walk.

3. AMERICAN ROBIN

In folklore, if you see an American robin during the winter, that means spring is coming soon. This flying sign of spring has a bright-red chest that makes it one of the most recognizable birds on this list. Its favorite foods are berries (yum!) and worms (gross!), and it loves taking baths. You're most likely to spot an American robin jumping around on the ground, looking for a berry snack or for a puddle to splash in.

4. BLACK-CAPPED CHICKADEE

The black-capped chickadee is the most common kind of chickadee in North America. It's a small bird with a very round body and a big head that makes it look like a flying puffball. Both male and female chickadees have olive-gray feathers, bright-white cheeks, and a distinctive patch of black feathers on their head that looks like a hat. How do you spot one on your next birding expedition? Well, the chickadee is named after the song it sings! So, when you hear "chick-a-dee-dee-dee," pull your binoculars out and look for this round, little bird.

5. BLUE JAY

A blue jay is a bright-blue, medium-size bird with black markings on its face. Blue jays (also called just "jays") have longer feathers on their heads that perk up or lie flat as their emotions change. And they're definitely moody birds! They are very protective of their food and nests, so if you see one, enjoy their beauty, but don't get too close.

6. DOWNY WOODPECKER

If you see a bright-red spot on a tree, stop and look! It might be the head of a downy woodpecker. This bird has a white chest and black wings with white speckles. Its head is striped with white and black and has a bright-red patch of feathers. The downy woodpecker is the smallest species of North American woodpecker, but it's every bit as loud as its larger cousins. When it's looking for bugs to eat, it pecks trees so hard that it sounds like someone is knocking on a door.

7. EUROPEAN STARLING

Since arriving in North America, the European starling has become one of the most common birds on the entire continent. Its shiny, black body is scattered with iridescent green and purple feathers, and it has a very short tail and a pointed, yellow beak. These black birds are sometimes called "bully birds" because they like to group together and scare all of the other birds away from their meals. Luckily, they're only interested in seeds and insects, so they shouldn't bully you for your lunch!

8. NORTHERN CARDINAL

With its stunning red color and iconic black mask, the male northern cardinal is one of the most recognizable birds in North America. Some people call the cardinal "redbird" because of its famous red feathers. But what else makes it unique? Well, the northern cardinal is the state bird for not one but seven states, and it doesn't migrate for the winter like most birds. Because they stick around to winter with us, you're most likely to spot their red body when it's against a snowy background!

9. MOURNING DOVE

A mourning dove is a medium-size bird, and it's famous for its soothing voice and gentle cooing song. Its body is light-brownish yellow (a color called "buff"), but its wings are darker with black spots. Mourning doves are shy birds and might not come out of hiding if they feel nervous, but they enjoy being with their family. Doves like sitting close together, so be on the lookout for groups cuddling together when you're looking for these gentle birds.

10. RUBY-THROATED HUMMINGBIRD

The ruby-throated hummingbird may be the most challenging bird to spot on this list because they're super small and amazingly quick. This tiny bird is even smaller than a chickadee and has a bright-green back, a black band around its eyes, and an iridescent red neck. But the hummingbird isn't just pretty—it's also a master flyer! It can go up to sixty miles per hour when diving, hover midair, and even fly backward! They love drinking nectar to keep their energy up, so if you're watching a hummingbird feeder closely, don't look away, or you might miss a very cute visitor.

FLOWERS, GRASSES, AND WEEDS, OH MY!

When you're exploring outside, do you like to stop and pick flowers or leaves to take home? Or maybe you enjoy lying in the grass and breathing in the refreshing smell of the outdoors. Whether you're a collector, an observer, or a bit of both, you'll be surprised how many different kinds of plants are out there, even in what might seem like a boring lawn or park.

Here's a list of the most common flowers, grasses, and weeds that you might be able to spot and identify on your next botanical expedition.

WILD ONION

You know you've found wild onion the moment you break one of its long, flat stalks because it will instantly smell like—you guessed it—onions! The part of the plant that grows aboveground looks like tall and thin blades of grass, but the rest of it hides in the earth. Wild onions spread really quickly and aren't bothered in the least by most weed killers, so if you consider this tiny vegetable a weed, you'll have to dig up a lot of tiny onions to get rid of it.

DANDELION

Dandelions are bright-yellow flowers that are usually considered a weed, and they can have roots fifteen feet long that make them a pain to pull up. After they've bloomed, they transform into white puffballs with a seed at the end of each fluff, and the fluff carries the seed off with the wind. Some people think that you can make a wish come true if you blow a dandelion's fuzz away, so think of some wishes to make next time you identify a dandelion!

WILD VIOLET

Wild violets are small purple flowers with five petals and large, heart-shaped green leaves. They enjoy the shade, but the adult plants can survive in many places. Because they're so tough and grow quickly, some people consider them to be a weed rather than a wildflower. But other people love violets because they can bloom in dozens of colors and pretty up a garden bed or pot. And did you know that the ancient Greeks saw violets as a symbol of love? So whether you love them or hate them, see if you can spot some wild violets tucked low to the ground next time you're on a walk, and if you do, pick a few for a loose, wildflower bouquet.

BACHELOR BUTTONS

Bachelor buttons are special because they're one of the very few flowers that are naturally blue. They grow in clusters on long, thin stalks that have a bright-blue flower that looks like a blue dandelion. They get their fun name because, back in the day, bachelors would put these flowers in their jacket's buttonhole as a sign that they were looking for someone to marry.

Next time you're on a lawn, examine the grass carefully and look for a stalk with a blue tint and blades that look like boats at the ends. If you see it, then you're probably looking at Kentucky bluegrass! What we think of as plain old grass is actually a whole genus, or large scientific category, that contains hundreds of different species of grasses. Over time, Kentucky bluegrass became the favorite species for lawns, and it won out over the other species because it's easy to take care of and has a beautiful blue tint. But Kentucky bluegrass isn't even from Kentucky! Like most grasses, it's originally from Europe.

DID YOU KNOW?

The science of identifying and classifying plants is called botany, but did you know that in botany there's actually no such thing as a weed? A weed is just a plant that most gardeners don't want around, either because it bothers other plants or because it's super tough to get rid of. So if you're out on a botanical expedition and spot a dandelion, the most common "weed," you'll know that, scientifically, it's just a flower like any other.

THE TEN-MINUTE VOLCANO

Every second, there are chemicals interacting around us and even inside our bodies. These reactions are usually too subtle for us to notice, but sometimes we can see them if we combine the right chemicals. In this experiment, you'll see what happens when vinegar and baking soda react to one another and make a lot of carbon dioxide. You can do this science experiment outside if it's a nice day or in a big bowl or sink inside. (Warning: it could get messy, in the best way!)

MATERIALS

- **2 (16-ounce) plastic cups**
- **½ cup vinegar**
- **⅔ cup dish soap**
- **Food coloring in any color**
- **Modeling clay (optional)**
- **4 tablespoons baking soda**
- **⅔ cup water**

INSTRUCTIONS

1. Mix the vinegar, dish soap, and 2 to 3 drops of food coloring in a 16-ounce cup. If you're using modeling clay to decorate, now is the time to mold it into the base of a volcano around the cup.

2. In a separate cup, mix the baking soda and water.

3. Pour the baking soda into the cup of vinegar, dish soap, and food coloring.

4. Stand back and watch what happens!

THE BOUNCIEST BUBBLES EVER

Blowing bubbles is super fun—until they pop! Bubbles are mostly made of water, so their surface is very delicate, especially once the water starts to evaporate. Even though you can't make a bubble last forever (boo!), you can make it last a little longer by adding other ingredients to the basic soapy formula (woo-hoo!). Whip out a bowl and a bubble wand, and we'll show you how to make bubbles that last longer and are tough enough to bounce in your hand.

MATERIALS

- **Small bowl**
- **¼ cup water**
- **2 tablespoons granulated sugar**
- **1 tablespoon dish soap**
- **Bubble wand, or wire or pipe cleaner bent in the shape of a wand**
- **Pair of latex or rubber gloves**

INSTRUCTIONS

1. In a bowl, add the water and sugar. Stir until the sugar completely dissolves.

2. Add the dish soap and mix gently.

3. Dip your bubble wand into the mixture and blow into the wand to form a bubble.

4. While wearing your gloves, dip your hands in the bubble solution, and then try to catch the bubble on your hand. Count how many times you can bounce the bubble before it pops!

PAINT YOUR OWN DAISIES

While adventuring, you've probably found beautiful flowers in different colors like red, blue, pink, and a bunch more. There are so many colors of flowers out in the world naturally, but what if you could make your very own custom color for a flower? Well, with some water, food coloring, and a little bit of patience, you can turn a flower into your own vibrant masterpiece. So go ahead and find some white flowers, and let's unleash your inner floral artist!

MATERIALS

- **3 (16-ounce) clear plastic cups**
- **Water**
- **Food coloring**
- **Scissors**
- **3 light-colored flowers, like daisies or white carnations**

INSTRUCTIONS

1. Fill each glass with water and mix in 3 to 5 drops of food coloring. Bonus tip: a flower soaks up warm water more quickly than cold water, so use slightly warm water for speedier absorption.

2. Using the scissors, make a slanted cut at least 1 inch from the bottom of two of the flower stems. Place each flower in its own cup of water.

3. For the third flower, cut the stem lengthwise and stop a little below the flower to make two halves. Place each half in differently colored cups of water.

4. Let sit overnight. In the morning, you'll wake up to a beautiful bouquet of flowers you colored yourself! Which do you like best—the one-colored flowers or the two-colored flower?

RAIN CLOUD IN A JAR

Imagine a big, fluffy rain cloud in the distance. These giant puffballs are made up of billions of tiny drops of water, and when the drops get heavy, they fall to the earth, and that's what we call rain. Want to get a closer look at this phenomenon? Let's gather up a few materials, build a miniature cloud, and start making our own rain!

MATERIALS

- **Medium glass jar**
- **Water**
- **Shaving cream**
- **Food coloring of any color**
- **Pipette (optional, if the food coloring doesn't have a dropper)**

INSTRUCTIONS

1. Fill the jar with water until it's three-quarters full.

2. Add shaving cream to completely cover the water.

3. Place 3 to 4 drops of food coloring on top of your shaving cream cloud using the food coloring dropper or a pipette.

4. Watch your colorful raindrops sprinkle down from your cloud!

RAINY DAY ACTIVITY

THE MAGICAL BENDY CANDY CANE

Candy canes are so sweet, minty, and . . . bendy? That's right! By adding a little bit of heat (ask a grown-up to help with the oven), you can transform hard candy canes into soft, shapeable sweets. You can stretch, flex, and twist your candy cane into a cat, a tree, an alien, or any other shape imaginable. You won't have too long to twist up your candy cane before it cools—race a friend and see how many creations each of you can make before the candy hardens too much to shape.

MATERIALS

- **Oven**
- **Cookie sheet**
- **Roll of parchment paper**
- **6 candy canes**
- **Timer**

INSTRUCTIONS

1. Preheat the oven to 250°F (121°C).

2. Line the cookie sheet with parchment paper and place the candy canes on the cookie sheet.

3. Bake for 8 to 10 minutes, checking the candy around 8 minutes. The candy canes will get a little puffy but shouldn't lose their shape.

4. Take the candy out of the oven and move the parchment paper with the candy canes onto a working surface, like a kitchen counter.

5. Let the candy cool off until warm to the touch.

6. Quickly twist the candy canes into new shapes like a bow, your favorite animal, or letters to spell out a special message. If the candy gets too stiff or you want to rework your shape, just reheat it in the oven and follow steps 1 through 3 again.

SIMPLE PAPER AIRPLANES
AND WHY THEY FLY

If you've ever been in a plane, you know they're like an enormous tin can. The Boeing 737, one of the most popular planes, seats up to 162 people, and it can weigh as much as 175,000 pounds. So how can something so big and so heavy possibly fly?

Well, making a plane fly is all about controlling force. Force is energy you use to make something move. When you kick a soccer ball, lift your backpack, or push a drawer closed, you are creating force to move that ball, backpack, and drawer. Airplanes fly by balancing four super-important forces: lift, thrust, drag, and weight. Pilots use the plane's wings and its engines to control these four forces that push the plane up and forward.

It takes a lot of training to become a pilot, but you can experiment with flight on a miniature level right now by building your own fleet of planes. You can build them all and race them through the sky to see which one can fly the highest, farthest, and fastest (and yes, add style points for the best decorations!).

MATERIALS

- **8.5 by 11-inch paper**
- **Tape or glue stick**
- **Markers or colored pencils for decorating (optional)**
- **Pencil**
- **Ruler**

SIMPLE: THE ARROW

1. Take an 8.5 by 11-inch sheet of paper and fold it in half lengthwise. Then unfold the paper.

2. Lay the paper on a flat surface and choose one of the short edges to be the top of your paper.

3. The top of your paper has two corners and a crease running down the middle. Fold both of the top corners in toward the center line (the points of each corner will meet at the center crease). When done correctly, the top of the paper will be angled symmetrically on both sides and look like a triangle sitting on top of a box.

4. Take another look at your paper. Notice how the box has four corners, two at the bottom and two at the top, just below the bottom of the triangle.

5. Like you did in step 3, fold the top corners of the box toward the center of the paper. The corners will meet at the center line, and the top sides of the triangle will also meet and lay right against each other. Once you've done this fold, your paper will start looking like an arrowhead.

6. Now fold the plane in half lengthwise. If both sides of the planes are symmetrical, then the sides should line up exactly when you fold it in half. Each half will be a wing for your plane!

7. Lay your paper on a flat surface and see how it looks like a right triangle with a missing corner. The paper has one short side, one long side that's straight, and one long side that's angled. In the next step, we're going to make both of the long sides line up.

8. Folding one wing at a time, fold the angled side down toward the long straight side and line them up so that both sides are parallel and form a straight line.

9. Once the sides are lined up straight, make a crease all the way down the plane.

10. Flip the plane to its opposite side (the one with the wing you haven't folded yet), and repeat steps 8 and 9 for the other wing. When both wings are folded, your plane will look like the long part of a very narrow men's tie.

11. Unfold the wings. The wings of your plane now look like an arrow and the plane's body (the part you pinch) will look like a tall and narrow right triangle.

12. Let it fly!

> **PRO TIP:**
> When you throw your plane, angle it up a little and see what happens!

INTERMEDIATE: THE FLOATING BEE

1. Lay your 8.5 by 11-inch paper on a flat surface horizontally (the long edges will be the top and bottom, and the short edges will be the sides).

2. Fold your paper in half, bringing the short sides together, and then unfold the paper.

3. Look at the paper's two top corners. Fold the top corners down to the center crease (the points of the corners will meet along the center line). After you've folded both corners, you will have two angled sides at the top of your paper, and the whole paper will look like a triangle with its base sitting on top of a long, slim rectangle.

4. Notice the line formed below the base of the triangle and the top of the rectangle. Also notice the perpendicular crease line.

5. Fold the top point of the triangle down to the line where the base of the triangle meets the top of the rectangle. The triangle's point should be right above the center crease line. Once you've lined it up, make a crease.

6. Now, your paper will look like an isosceles trapezoid sitting on top of a long, slim rectangle. Take a second to find the two angled sides of the top trapezoid and the center crease running down the paper's center. They'll be important in the next step!

7. Look at the left side of the paper and the angled side of the trapezoid. With this next fold, we want to line that angled side along the center crease.

8. Fold the left angled side toward the center line and crease the fold. You've just made the first wing!

9. Repeat this fold for the right side. When folded correctly, the right and left angled sides will lay right beside each other on the center line, and both wings will be symmetrical. With this step, your buzzy friend will really start taking shape!

10. When looking down at your paper, see how there's two long angled edges and two ends (one is wide and the other is narrow). Arrange the paper on a flat surface so the wide end of the paper is the bottom, the narrow part is the top, and the angled edges are the sides. Make sure you're looking at the side of the plane where the wings can open up to you!

11. Notice how the wings form two small triangles, one at the top that's upside down and one at the bottom that's right side up. In the next step, we'll be folding the top of the plane and the top triangle will be important.

12. Fold the top of the plane backward (away from you) so that half of the top triangle is folded back (only a little bit of the triangle will still be visible to you!).

13. Fold the plane in half lengthwise so the wings mirror each other. You'll notice that the top section that you just folded backward is now on the underside of the plane.

14. With the plane on its side, fold one wing down about half an inch and make a crease.

15. Flip the plane over and fold the second wing down so it matches the first one.

16. Now your wings are done, but you'll notice that the inner sides of the plane's body (the section in between the wings) do not stay together. For this plane design, we'll want to seal the inside of the body using a glue stick or a little bit of tape.

17. Once sealed, your bee is ready to drift! Just like a real bumblebee, this plane stays in the air for a long time—guess how long your bee will stay airborne, and then time it to see if you're right.

ADVANCED: THE TRICK PILOT

1. Lay your 8.5 by 11-inch paper vertically on a flat surface (the rectangle's short edges will be the top and bottom and the rectangle's long edges will be the sides).

2. Fold the paper in half downward and toward you to create a crease that will run across the middle of the paper and be parallel to the short edges of the paper.

3. Now that the paper is folded in half, your paper will look like a smaller, horizontal rectangle (the long sides are the top and bottom of the rectangle). For the next step, make sure that the creased edge is the top of the rectangle and the bottom part is the side that can be opened back up to the original sheet of paper.

4. Look at the short right edge of the rectangle. Next, look at the bottom right corner. Notice how there's a top sheet of paper and a bottom one. In the next step, we'll just be folding the top sheet.

5. Fold a diagonal crease that will make the rectangle's short edge line up with the rectangle's top edge. Take the bottom right corner and bend it upward so the short edge lines up with the top edge. When done correctly, you'll notice that a diagonal crease now runs from the top right corner all the way to the bottom of the rectangle.

6. Repeat step 5 for the left side, making sure to only fold the top sheet and line up the short edge with the top of the rectangle. If the paper looks like an envelope after folding the left side, then you're on the right track!

7. Notice how your paper now looks like an envelope (a rectangle with an upside-down triangle inside of that rectangle). Look at the bottom point of the upside-down triangle.

8. Take the top right corner of the paper and fold it down to meet the point of the upside-down triangle. The point of the top corner will touch the point of the triangle and form a diagonal crease.

9. Repeat step 8 for the left side. Now, both corner points will be beside each other. With both sides folded, your paper will look like a triangle sitting on top of a long, skinny rectangle.

10. Unfold both of the corners you just folded. You'll be back to the rectangle from step 3, but now you'll see two diagonal creases. These creases are important for the next step!

11. Look at the top right corner again. With the diagonal crease as a baseline, the corner will look like a triangle. Take the top right corner and fold it toward the diagonal crease so that the right edge of the triangle (the edge that's a part of the right side of the whole rectangle) lines up with the diagonal crease (or the "base" of the triangle).

12. Repeat step 11 for the top left corner, this time making sure that the left side of the triangle (the edge that's part of the left side of the whole rectangle) lines up with the diagonal crease (or the "base" of the triangle).

13. Now that both of the corners are folded down to their diagonal creases, fold along the diagonal creases again, making sure that the corners stay folded in. Your paper will look like an arrow on top plus a long, straight edge and two corners at the bottom.

14. Look at the pointed top of your paper. From that top point, run your eyes down and find a pointed flap of paper (it will look like a diamond shape popping out from underneath the diagonal folds you just made).

15. Fold the pointed flap upward. It will now look like a little triangle, and its point and angled sides will line up with the top point and angled sides of the whole paper.

16. Turn the paper over so all the folds you just made are lying against the flat surface, and the back of the plane is now faceup toward you.

17. Fold the plane in half and crease down the middle. Each side is a wing, and the wings should line up symmetrically over the crease. After folding in half, the paper will look like a right triangle that's missing its lower point.

18. Without unfolding the paper, position the plane so that the right angle is on the bottom left, the missing point of the triangle is on the bottom right, and the angled edge is on the right side.

19. Look at the bottom side of the paper (the side between the right angle and the missing point) and divide the space into three equal segments with a pencil going from left to right. Put your finger at the end of the first segment (the one closest to the paper's vertical edge) and make a mark.

20. Now look at the point in the top left (the point made by the vertical edge and the angled edge). Use a pencil and make a mark on the angled edge, close to the top point. We recommend making the mark about half a centimeter away from the top point.

21. You should now have a mark at the top on the angled side and one at the bottom about a third of the way from the vertical edge. Connect these two points using a ruler and pencil. You now have a diagonal line.

22. Fold along the line you just drew. Then flip the plane over without unfolding your new crease.

23. Fold the second wing down so that it mirrors the opposite side. Your paper will now look similar to a kite with two long edges and two shorter ones.

24. Find the shortest of the four edges. This edge will become your plane's fins.

25. Take the short edge of one wing and fold it down. The crease should be parallel with the short edge, and the fin should be about as wide as your pinky. Do this step for both wings.

26. Finally, unfold the wings and fins. Make sure the wings are tilted up and the fins are pointed up. Throw your plane straight up into the air and see what happens. This plane is designed for tricks— see how many you can discover!

CHAPTER 2:

Let's Be Trailblazers!

Ah, the great outdoors. Whether you're enjoying a jaunt through the neighborhood park or trekking to a national park for a big-scale adventure, there's nothing like the smell of fresh air, the sound of wind in the trees, and the bigness of the wide-open sky above you. In this chapter, you'll find all the essentials you need to have a blast on a hike or camping trip, what exactly to do if trouble strikes, and how you can take care of the planet even when you're home. So grab your boots, your water bottle, and a backpack, and let's get outside!

THE HANDS-ON GIRL'S BACKPACK

Itching to dart outside to spend time in nature? Remember that you never need anything to step outside and go for a walk (other than permission and maybe a coat!), but if you're planning a longer hike or trip, consider packing up these supplies for a more easygoing time.

THE JAUNT-IN-THE-WOODS BACKPACK

There's nothing like a walk in the woods to make you feel great and boost your mood. And with just a few things tucked in your pack, you can trailblaze for longer and farther, even on the busiest days.

☐ **Water bottle**
☐ **Hiking boots**
☐ **Sunglasses or hat**
☐ **Compass**
☐ **Sunscreen**
☐ **Bug spray**
☐ **Raincoat (if it might rain)**

THE WEEKEND CAMPOUT BACKPACK

Ready for a big overnighter under the stars? You'll need to add a few things to your hiking backpack to stay comfortable and safe (and warm!), but even with the extra baggage in tow, you'll be surprised at just how simply you can cook, eat, and sleep when you're under the stars.

- [ ] **Tent**
- [ ] **Sleeping bag**
- [ ] **Firewood or camping stove**
- [ ] **Waterproof matches**
- [ ] **Newspaper**
- [ ] **Paper plates**
- [ ] **Spork**
- [ ] **Trash bag**
- [ ] **Paper towels**
- [ ] **Toilet paper**
- [ ] **Antibacterial wipes**
- [ ] **First aid kit**
- [ ] **Trail mix, hot dogs and buns, s'mores supplies, and your other campfire favorites**

CAMPING 101

Whether you're exploring the vast wilderness or just enjoying your own backyard, camping is the perfect way to add more sunlight, firelight, and starlight to a regular humdrum day. As soon as you spend your first night falling asleep in your cozy tent, listening to the crickets and night birds and waking up to a roaring campfire breakfast, you'll see what all the hype is about. But all that magic does start with some good planning. Knowing what and what not to bring on a trip can seem overwhelming (especially if you're going far from home!), but this section will break down the basics of what you'll want to wear, pack, and eat. There's even a list of important items at the end that you can use to double-check your supplies. So, get ready to take some notes and master this crash course in camping 101.

FUNCTION OVER FASHION

When roughing it outside, you'll want to sport some clothes that will make you as comfortable as possible (but not your pajamas, even though it's tempting!). The first thing to consider is actually fabric, not style, color, and cut like we usually start with when we're picking an outfit. It's best to skip cotton because it traps moisture, like sweat, and no one wants to be a damp camper. Look for clothes made from materials like polyester, wool, or any synthetic material that dries quickly. You'll also want items that you can layer or take off as you get hot or chilly, like an extra fleece jacket, raincoat, or long underwear.

Overall, your outfit should let you move easily and protect your body from bugs, ultraviolet rays from the sun, prickly plants, and so on. Wearing long pants and high socks will cover your skin and act as a barrier between you and nature's low-lying plant and insect life. Wild plants and creatures are awesome, but not when they're nipping at your ankles! A sturdy pair of shoes to go with your tall socks is also a must-have. You don't need top-of-the-line hiking boots; you just want shoes, like sneakers, that are comfortable to walk in and that cover your whole foot. To top everything off, put on a brimmed hat, like a baseball cap. A hat with a brim will give you a little bit of personal shade and add some nice style to your look.

And finally, remember your PJs for nighttime! Bring a light bottom layer of PJs, but then tuck a second layer of warm pants, a long-sleeve shirt, or a sweater next to your sleeping bag, since the temperature always drops at night, even in the summer. You'll feel better knowing that, if it gets too chilly near dawn, you can always slide on an extra-cozy sweater or pants and curl right back into your sleeping bag.

CAMPSITE ESSENTIALS

Traveling light is the trick to an easy camping trip, and your most essential items will be food, water, and shelter. If you don't want to cook in the wild, bring food that's ready to eat, like dried fruit, nuts, granola, or jerky. You'll also need a ton of water! Staying hydrated is the secret to feeling energetic and perky, instead of tired and wilting, so fill up several water jugs with clean water from home, which you can use to refill your water bottle. For shelter, pack your sleeping bag and pick out a tent that's big enough for you and your camping comrades. You'll all be cozy in the same tent, but you shouldn't be packed in like sardines—nobody likes an elbow to the face at 2 a.m., right?

A few other things that will keep you happy, comfortable, and safe are a first aid kit, hand sanitizer, soap, sunscreen, bug repellant, and a flashlight. Try finding mini versions of these items to keep your packing light. Also, depending on your campsite, you may want to bring a trash bag and some toilet paper!

MORE FOOD AND FUN

Camping isn't just about survival basics—we also want to have a ton of fun, which means bringing any extra goodies we can reasonably pack. What you choose to do on your camping trip is totally up to you and your friends. If you're most excited about cooking over a campfire, then don't forget the hot dogs, buns, toppings, and s'mores materials, or even try one of the recipes for more-gourmet grub on page 174. Is there a lake or stream nearby to swim in? Pack a swimsuit or even an inflatable float. Are you excited about spotting insects and wildlife? Don't forget your binoculars and maybe even a terrarium if you want to bring some insect specimens home. The best part about camping is that you get to do the outdoorsy things *you* like best, so don't be shy about telling the group what you want to add to the packing list. You'll always want to start with the essentials, but it's good to make your own mini list of extra stuff that can be piled in the car if there's enough space.

CAMPING ESSENTIALS AND EXTRAS CHECKLIST
CLOTHING ESSENTIALS

- [ ] **Long pants and high socks**
- [ ] **Sturdy and comfortable shoes**
- [ ] **Hat with a brim**
- [ ] **Pajamas**
- [ ] **Two layers of tops, one light and one warm**

CAMPSITE ESSENTIALS

- [ ] Tent
- [ ] Sleeping bag
- [ ] Battery-powered lamps or flashlights
- [ ] Extra batteries
- [ ] Water
- [ ] Nonperishable food
- [ ] Trash bag
- [ ] Sunscreen and insect repellant
- [ ] Toilet paper
- [ ] First aid kit
- [ ] Hand sanitizer and soap
- [ ] Firewood or camping stove
- [ ] Matches or lighter

COMFY AND FUN EXTRAS

- [ ] Camp chairs
- [ ] Extra blanket
- [ ] Binoculars
- [ ] Swimsuit
- [ ] Extra food, if cooking
- [ ] Disposable plates, utensils, and cups
- [ ] Fire-safe skillet, such as cast iron
- [ ] Salt, pepper, and cooking oil
- [ ] Oven mitt and fire-safe tongs
- [ ] Board games
- [ ] Books or magazines
- [ ] Deck of cards

GRAB A GROWN-UP!

TEN MINUTES WALKING THROUGH NATURE

A walk through a forest or field can seem like nothing special, especially if you've gone that way a million times before. But that's where the power of mindfulness and looking carefully at things can change everything. When you're out in nature, it's like you're transported to another realm, full of grasses, flowers, birds, bugs, rocks, and other stuff we miss out on when we're inside all day. A regular old log may not look like much, but if you look closer, you might spot a bird or squirrel, or even uncover a village of bugs camping out under the bark, living their own lives in their own way. If you aren't paying attention, you can miss nearly everything nature has to offer. So if you have even just ten minutes outside, what should you look for? Here are a few ideas to help you mindfully observe and enjoy nature. (And don't forget to check in with your grown-up or bring them along if you're going far or staying out long!)

1. CLOSE YOUR EYES AND LISTEN

What do you hear? Do you hear the wind blowing through the trees? Do you hear animals making sounds? If so, what type of sounds are they, and what type of animal do you think might be making them?

2. SEARCH FOR COOL-LOOKING PLANTS

If you find a weird-shaped plant that you've never seen before, study it closely and figure out what makes it unique. How many leaves does it have, and how would you describe their shape and color if you had to write it down? Then look it up when you get home to try to figure out what it is and why it might be growing there.

3. HOW MANY COLORS CAN YOU FIND?

If you're outside during the spring, you might be able to spot flowers or colorful berries, no matter what part of the world you live in. Count how many different colors you see, and every time you go back outside, try to beat your record. Make up your own color names if you feel like it—after all, there are trillions of colors out there.

4. GET UP CLOSE TO TREES

Trees come in every shape and size, and while it's fun to watch one for a few minutes, it's especially interesting to feel its bark and its leaves. Some tree bark may be rough and ridged, while others are smooth or peeling. Many leaves have sharp edges, or even pointy spikes, while some are soft and tender. Remember that you're not in a museum here—touch everything you see, as long as it looks safe!

5. WATCH A BUG VILLAGE

If you see a small or medium branch or log on the ground, roll it over to uncover what's underneath. Maybe there's a whole world of life under that old, rotten log. Bugs, worms, and slugs love the cool, wet environment down there, and you might see them crawling around, eating, sleeping, and running their own buggy errands just like we do. Watch them live a few minutes of their lives, but make sure you replace the log before you leave—it's their home.

6. COLLECT STONES

When you really get down and look, it's mind-blowing how many cool, weird, and totally different rocks there are out there. Scan the ground as you walk, or squat for a closer view, and scoop up any rocks with unique colors, or weird shapes, or ones that change color when dipped into water. Any rock that you think is an interesting specimen or that speaks to you is worth keeping.

7. CLIMB A TREE

Nature is full of ready-made tree forts, just waiting for someone like you to climb aboard. Make sure an adult is around before scaling any tree, just in case, but if you find a sturdy and safe one, climb on up and have a look around for a higher view. What can you see happening on the tree and around the tree from up there?

8. SPLASH IN A PUDDLE OR STREAM

Go for a walk after a big rainstorm and wear your rain boots so you can splash right into any puddles or streams. Before hopping in, stop for a second to scan the banks and see if you can spot any water-loving wildlife, like frogs, water bugs, or tadpoles.

9. GO OUTSIDE AT NIGHT

Going outside after dark, even in your own backyard, opens up a whole new way to explore nature. Different animals come out at night and make different noises. Stand still and listen for five minutes and count all the different noises you hear. At night you'll also be able to spot some stars—can you name any of them? (To learn more star names, check out The Stars and Their Names, page 5.)

10. STARGAZE

Can you spot any of the constellations (see page 6)? If you want to explore the night sky more, go to www.in-the-sky.org, type in your town's name, and you'll find lists and maps of all the constellations, planets, comets, and more that are visible from your exact location.

11. BRING A FRIEND

Walking through nature by yourself is peaceful, but sometimes it's fun to have someone to point things out to, and to both guess about what's what. You can also make it a game of I-Spy and take turns naming what you see. Who can spot the most flowers? How many different types of trees can each of you find? Which one of you can collect the best stones?

FISHING 101

The art of fishing has nourished and entertained people for thousands of years. Ancient images found in Africa, Asia, and Europe show people fishing as early as 2000 BCE. Although a lot of human technology has advanced since then, fishing hasn't changed all that much—it still comes down to casting a line or net into the water and patiently waiting for a nibble. And while there are tons of gadgets, fancy rods, and colorful bait you can buy these days, you don't really need much if you want to dip your toes into a new fishing hobby. So if you're curious about what's so fun about fishing, then check out this guide, grab your grown-up, and get ready for fishing to capture your heart hook, line, and sinker.

BEFORE YOU FISH

CHECK FISHING LICENSE REQUIREMENTS

Depending on where you live and how old you are, you may need a special license to start fishing. The licenses help prevent overfishing by keeping track of how many people are fishing in your area. Even though getting a license sounds complicated, they're actually super easy to get, and most areas let you buy one online in just a few minutes. Even better, a lot of states let people under the age of sixteen fish without a license, so check out your local game and wildlife agency and see if you even need one.

SCOUT FISHING LOCATIONS

A good fishing location needs to give you two things: 1. fish in the water and 2. permission to fish there. Make sure you always have both!

GET TO KNOW THE (FISHY) LOCALS

Fish are a lot like people—different fish like different foods. So once you've figured out what kind of fish can be found at your fishing spot, you'll want to do some research to figure out what bait you should bring and how you should move that bait (for instance, if the fish lives near the bottom of the water, you'll need to let the bait sink!). One of the best sources for fishing advice is your local sporting goods store, since people who work there are likely to be familiar with all the nearby watering holes, what's in them, and what should be on the menu. But you can also research online by searching for something like "best bait for bass in Virginia" or "fishing the James River in April" and seeing what other anglers are recommending in articles, forums, and YouTube videos.

EQUIPMENT AND SETUP

CHOOSING A REEL AND ROD

A great beginner fishing rod is a spinning reel and rod combo. With this pole, the reel is connected to the rod, which prevents any chance of your reel coming off. You may also want to get a rod with a closed-face reel. This kind of reel has a cover over the spool of fishing line, which decreases the chance of tangling and makes casting easier. When we talk about casting later on, we'll be describing how to cast with a closed-faced reel.

PACKING YOUR TACKLE BOX

The tackle box is your fishing tool kit. Most tackle boxes have plenty of bait, extra hooks and weights, scissors to cut fishing line, and pliers to remove hooks from fish. But if you're just starting out, you don't need one of the fancy boxes with hundreds of tiny little cubbies in them. You can repurpose any bag you already have, but just be sure to keep your hooks and bait separated in little plastic baggies or containers so they don't get tangled.

TYING A KNOT

You need a secure knot to attach your hook, and most anglers use the clinch knot. To attach a hook with a clinch knot, start by feeding the fishing line through the loop at the top of the hook. Then wrap the short end of line up along the long end five times. You should now have a loop below the wrapped section. Take the short end and pass it through the first loop. Now you have a new, larger loop. Pass the end upward through the new loop. Finally, pull both ends of line to tighten the knot.

BAITING YOUR HOOK

The goal here is to run your hook lengthwise through the bait. So, if you have a worm, the hook will line up with the length of the worm, not the width. Take your hook and carefully stick it through the bait. Then work the bait higher on the hook. Since hooks are crazy sharp, it's a great idea to let someone with more experience walk you through the process a few times.

CASTING AND CATCHING

CASTING WITH A CLOSED-FACE REEL

Hold the handle of the rod in front of you with both hands and look for the button on the reel. Use your thumb on your dominant hand to push the button and hold it down. Your line is now ready to cast and will let out more line once you release the button. Still holding the button down, turn your arms and torso to the side, like you're winding up to throw a baseball. You'll always cast from the side and never over your head. This way, you'll always know where your hook is. Swing your body back toward the center and, when you're about to face front again, let go of the button. Your line will unravel and fly in the direction that the tip of your rod was pointing toward when you let go. Casting straight and far takes a lot of practice, so keep casting and reeling back in until the movement seems more natural.

CATCHING AND RELEASING A FISH

Once your hook is in the water, let it sink a little deeper into the water, then *slowly* turn the handle on your reel to bring the line back in. Fishing is a waiting game, so you have to be patient. When a fish bites, your rod will bow downward, and you'll notice that something seems to be pulling on the line. As soon as you see this, quickly jerk your rod up to lock in the hook and then reel in normally. The fish will put up a fight, so hang tough! When the fish becomes visible, have a friend scoop it up with a net. If you want to touch it, make sure your hands are wet first and hold the fish sideways, gently, watching for any sharp scales or fins. Never dangle it by the line—that doesn't feel very good to the little guy! Keep the fish out of the water only as long as you need to get a good look at him, and unhook him. To throw him back, remove the hook with your pliers or, if the fish swallowed the hook, cut the line and tie on a new hook for your next cast.

HOW TO GET UNLOST
IN THE WOODS

If you ever get lost when you're camping, the first thing to remember is the famous old saying: "You're not lost; it's the camp that's lost." As long as you sit tight and let the camp and your friends there find you, you'll be unlost much quicker than you would've thought possible.

As soon as you notice that you're not sure where you are, try to remind yourself of three things:

1. You're not nearly as far from camp as you think you are.
2. Your friends are going to find you soon.
3. You can help your friends find you by signaling to them.

Start by taking a few deep breaths. The next thing you should do is get on a hill, or climb a tree, or find another high lookout, and search for some kind of landmark near the camp. If you don't see any landmarks, look for the smoke of the campfire. Instead of wandering around and probably getting more lost, try to stay in one place. Every once in a while, shout as loud as you can—most of the time, you're still within earshot of your friends!

While you stay in one spot, you can also work on signaling to your friends. The best way to do this is to send a distress signal, which is usually a smoke signal. Make two very small fires (see page 50 for how to build a fire) and then smother them with green leaves and rotten wood so the flame goes out but they start to smoke. Try to keep them at least fifty feet apart, or the wind will blow them together and they'll end up looking like one big smoke signal. Two smokes are like an SOS signal, which tells other people that you're in trouble.

Your friends will be able to track you down by the smoke, so just sit tight by the fire and wait for them to turn up. And before you know it, you'll be back at the campsite toasting s'mores and laughing about it all together!

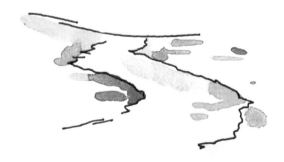

GRAB A GROWN-UP!

THE S'MORES SMORGASBORD OF YOUR STARLIT DREAMS

S'mores are amazing. But what's even more amazing than a regular s'more? S'mores with hazelnut spread swiped under the chocolate. S'mores with peanut butter cups squished between the graham crackers. S'mores with *cookies* for crackers. S'mores with cookies stacked on cookies, marshmallows stacked on marshmallows, and chocolate fudge to glue it all together. That's because hands-on girls think outside the graham square, and they know that whatever they love, in life and in desserts, they can mix it all together and turn it into their dream experience.

Makes 1 s'more

STRUCTURE

- **Graham crackers**
- **Cinnamon graham crackers**
- **Chocolate chip cookies**
- **Girl Scout cookies (any kind!)**
- **Oreos**
- **Vanilla wafers**
- **Gingersnaps**
- **Brownies**
- **Doughnuts**
- **Waffles**
- **Pita chips**
- **Saltines**
- **Pretzel crisps**
- **Ridged potato chips**
- **Ritz crackers**
- **Broken waffle cones**
- **Biscuits**

GOOEYNESS

- **Milk chocolate bar**
- **White chocolate bar**
- **Cookies-and-cream bar**
- **Mint chocolate**
- **Peanut butter cup**
- **Candy bar (any kind!)**
- **Hazelnut spread**
- **Chocolate fudge**
- **Cookie dough**
- **Chocolate kiss**
- **Caramel**
- **Peanut butter**
- **Jelly (any kind!)**
- **Lemon curd**
- **Honey**

GLUE

- **Marshmallows (keep it simple and roastable!)**

SURPRISE

- **Ice cream**
- **Whipped cream**
- **Sprinkles**
- **Chopped almonds**
- **Chopped walnuts**
- **M&Ms**
- **Gummy bears**
- **Jelly beans**

- **Toasted coconut flakes**
- **Strawberries**
- **Banana**
- **Pineapple**
- **Pear**
- **Dried cherries**
- **Brie**
- **Bacon**

INSTRUCTIONS

1. Choose your favorite structure, gooeyness, and surprise pieces from the lists above. If your gooey element is something that needs to be melted, such as a chocolate bar, stack it on top of one of your structural pieces and place near the heat of the fire, such as on a rock or log.

2. Skewer a marshmallow on a stick and roast near the coals of the fire, where it's hottest but also least likely to catch on fire. Make sure you have a grown-up nearby, just in case there's a fire flare-up.

3. Once your marshmallow is browned on the outside and soft enough that it's beginning to fall off the stick, place it on the melted half of the s'mores and use the other half of your structural element to squeeze it down as you pull out the stick.

4. Give your s'more a good smash and snack away!

HOW TO BUILD A FIRE

What's better than a summer night outdoors? A summer night outdoors with a blazing fire! As any hiker, camper, or backyard explorer knows, sitting around a roaring fire with your friends is the best reward after a long day outside. You can cook yummy food over a fire, tell your friends all about what you did that day, and most importantly, make s'mores! (For the best s'mores ever, go to The S'mores Smorgasbord of Your Starlit Dreams on page 48.)

Fires are also important for other reasons. When it's cold out, a warm fire can help toast you up and keep you from shivering. After a day swimming or being outside in the rain, a fire can dry you so you're not soggy and waterlogged all night. And if you get lost in the woods, fires can even help your friends track you down. (See How to Get Unlost in the Woods on page 46.) But the other secret thing about fires? They're super fun to build! If you have an adult nearby and just a few simple materials, you can test your fire-starter skills and see just how much fun it is to spark your own flame.

Fires are built with three main components: tinder, kindling, and fuel wood. Tinder is what you use to light the first flames; the best types of tinder are dry leaves, pine needles, or newspaper, which quickly catch fire. Kindling is usually small sticks or twigs that help the first flames grow and spread into a larger fire. Finally, fuel wood is the larger pieces of wood that you add to keep your fire burning for hours. Once you know how to combine these three fire ingredients together in the right way, you'll be the go-to fire whisperer at camp.

MATERIALS

- **Handful of dry leaves, pine needles, or newspaper**
- **5 to 6 small dry sticks or twigs**
- **7 to 8 medium branches or small logs**
- **Matches**

INSTRUCTIONS

1. Choose a flat, dry spot on the ground, at least 10 to 20 feet from any overhanging trees. Clear away any debris, such as loose stones or damp leaves.

2. Grab a handful of your dry leaves, pine needles, or newspaper and place it in the middle of your selected spot.

3. Stack 5 to 6 twigs or sticks loosely over the top of the tinder. You can test the dryness of your twigs or sticks by snapping them in half. If they snap easily, they're dry, but if they bend, they're probably too wet to burn well.

4. Add 3 to 4 larger branches or logs at different angles (some leaning on each other) to create a mini pyramid on top of your tinder and kindling. Be careful not to push down too hard and smash the leaves and sticks underneath. We want to give the fire room to breathe.

5. Strike a match and place it next to the tinder until it catches fire.

6. Gently blow on the flame to help it get enough oxygen to continue burning (but don't blow it out!). As the fire spreads from the tinder to the kindling, the flames will grow.

7. After 5 to 10 minutes, once your branches or logs start burning, you'll have a cozy fire roaring away. Then just keep adding more fuel wood to keep it going as long as you want.

8. Remember never to walk away from a fire, and when you're ready to extinguish it, throw plenty of water on it until there are no sparks or embers glowing among the ashes.

FIVE KNOTS AND HOW TO USE THEM

When you think of ancient technology, what comes to mind? Maybe stone tools or rough wheels, but what about knots? Artifacts show that people were using knots way before stone tools, and we still use them all the time today (just look down at someone's sneakers!). Knots are an incredible example of human ingenuity, and we've invented thousands of kinds of knots since the prehistoric days, each with its own pros and cons. Tying a knot is like tying yourself into a connection with the millions of people who tied that same exact knot before you—isn't it crazy to think about that each time you tie your sneakers? But even beyond all that history, knowing how to tie a few sturdy knots is just about the handiest thing you can learn to do. Here are five of the most common knots, how to make them, and why they may be useful to you:

1. SQUARE KNOT

Although not the strongest knot, the square knot is commonly used to connect two ropes. To make it, first take one end from each rope and place the right end over the left. Then cross the right rope under the left one (like you're doing the first step of tying your shoe). Repeat this process again, placing the right end over the left and then crossing the right under the left. Finally, pull the end of each rope to tighten the knot. This is the one knot you want to have in your back pocket at all times, since it's so easy and simple.

2. OVERHAND KNOT

The overhand knot is found at the ends of a rope and is used to keep the rope from unraveling. It's easy and exactly what you want if you have a fraying rope. Just make a loop at the rope's end and then stick the end of the rope through the loop. Pull the end of the rope, and it's done.

3. SLIPKNOT

Slipknots are adjustable loops that are also easy to completely unknot. Start by picking a point along the rope somewhere between the rope's end and its midpoint. At the place you choose, make a loop and hold it in one hand. Then reach your other hand through the loop and grab the longer section of rope. Bring it through the loop and pull the shorter end of the loop to tighten the knot. You'll see that you can slide this knot up and down, making it infinitely adjustable to whatever you're using it for.

4. BOWLINE KNOT

This is a strong knot that's speedy to tie and untie, so it's really handy for securing things like hammocks. Begin with a loop, crossing one end of rope over the rest of the rope. Then bring the rope under and through the loop. Next, bring the end of the rope behind the rope leading into the original loop and wrap it back toward the front to pass it through the loop. Pull the end down to tighten the knot.

5. CLOVE HITCH

The clove hitch is used to attach a rope to something stationary quickly, like attaching a climber's rope to an anchor point when rock climbing. Wrap the rope around the object once and cross the rope so that an X faces you. Hold one end of the rope to the side and then wrap the other end around the object again. Take the end you just moved and bring it under the section you're holding to the side. Run the end of that rope through the lower loop (a bottom point of the X) and finally pull to tighten.

FIRST AID FOR QUICK THINKERS

If someone's injured, what do you do? The best thing to do is look for an adult, like a parent or group leader, but it's also important to know how to take care of minor injuries yourself so you'll always feel safe and prepared for the unexpected. Knowing your way around a basic first aid kit will help you think quick if you're ever in a literal scrape. Here's what your first aid kit should have:

- [ ] Adhesive bandages: covers small scrapes and cuts
- [ ] Antibiotic ointment: for minor cuts
- [ ] Cloth tape and absorbent compresses: used to make larger bandages
- [ ] Antiseptic wipes: cleans injuries
- [ ] Aspirin or pain medicine: alleviates pain, like muscle aches or headaches
- [ ] Instant cold press: cools body and reduces swelling
- [ ] Gloves: protects your hands while treating someone else
- [ ] Hydrocortisone: reduces itching, redness, and swelling from things like insect bites or rashes
- [ ] Gauze roll: another type of bandage that you wrap around an injury
- [ ] Gauze pads: the same as a gauze roll but precut into patches
- [ ] Tweezers: pulls out things like splinters
- [ ] Thermometer: checks a person's temperature
- [ ] Emergency first aid guide: a booklet explaining basic first aid

With just one compact little case, you'll be able to treat most of the injuries you might run into while camping. Here are the five most common hurts you might have to heal on the go:

BUGBITES AND STINGS

A bad bugbite can feel insanely itchy and annoying, but a little first aid can give some amazing relief. Start with a cold compress to cool off those hot bites. The cold will calm any pain, swelling, or redness. Once the area has calmed down, dab on some hydrocortisone to help counteract any itchiness. Keep using the hydrocortisone as directed on its packaging until the itchiness is gone.

SCRAPES AND CUTS

Small cuts and scrapes happen all the time and are really easy to treat. If there's bleeding, apply pressure with a clean towel or cloth until the bleeding stops. Next, gently wash the area with warm water and antiseptic wipes and pat dry. Put on some antibacterial ointment and cover the spot with a bandage. For the next few days, change the bandage at least once a day, but if you're sweating, swimming, or just getting extra dirty on the trail, you might have to change your bandage a few times a day. But otherwise, patching up a cut is not much different than when you're at home.

MINOR BURNS

One of the best parts of being outside is sitting around a roaring fire, but all that roaring means it's all too easy to catch a flame the wrong way. And we all know how much even a small burn can hurt. Minor burns will be smaller than three inches in diameter and look like a red sunburn. First, cool off the burn with a cool (not cold) compress. The burned area will swell, so take off tight things around the burn, like rings. The burn will also have dried your skin, so put on a moisturizing lotion and gently wrap the burn with a loose bandage, like a gauze pad bound with cloth tape. Blisters might form as the burn heals, but don't pop them! They'll go away with time, and they'll just hurt much worse if you poke at them.

Minor burns are easy to soothe and wrap up this way, but remember that a burn that is very dark and larger than three inches across needs to be treated quickly by a medical professional.

NOSEBLEEDS

Blood can flow out of your nose for all kinds of reasons, but there's no need to panic, even if you're far from camp. All you need to do is stop the flow. Start by pinching your nostrils shut and sitting up straight. You can sit on a log if you're on the trail, or just stand, as long as you can stand still for a while. Lean forward a little and keep pinching for ten to fifteen minutes without letting go. This will give your body time to dry out that flow. While waiting, breathe through your mouth and pull loose any tight clothing around your neck. You can also place a cold compress on your forehead and around your neck, if you have one. Once the blood has stopped, try not to breathe through your nose or blow your nose for the rest of the day. It may feel gross, but it will give your sniffer some time to heal!

SPLINTERS

We all know how annoying and painful a splinter can be, and out in the wild, there's a lot more wood to catch splinters from! A splinter can also cramp your outdoors fun if it's someplace inconvenient, like on your foot when you're hiking. But even though you're outside and sweatier than usual, the most important thing is to keep your hands and the splinter area very clean to avoid later infection. So first, before you start picking at it, clean your hands with soap and water or hand sanitizer. Clean your tweezers the same way. Gently grab the end of the splinter with the tweezers and pull it out slowly. If the splinter is deeply embedded, you may need to try to pinch the skin surrounding it to slide it closer to the surface. Once the splinter is gone, wash the area again, smooth on some antibacterial ointment, and wrap the area in a bandage to keep dirt out.

DIY SLINGSHOT

A slingshot is basically a miniature catapult you can fit in your back pocket, and it's a ridiculously fun tool to practice your sharpshooting. On the next rainy day, you can design and construct one to practice your shot indoors or to have it ready for some outdoor target practice when the weather clears. Slingshots are amazing because of their simple yet powerful design. They pack so much power into each shot that they were used to hunt, defend, and attack before there were more sophisticated weapons. Here's a simple yet mighty version that you can use to show off your wicked aim.

MATERIALS

- **"Y"-shaped branch, preferably from a hardwood tree like an oak**
- **Scissors**
- **Scrap leather**
- **Large rubber bands**
- **Hot glue gun**
- **Yarn (optional)**
- **Small round projectiles, such as paper balls, foil balls, dried chickpeas, or marshmallows**

INSTRUCTIONS

1. Find a forked tree branch that makes a "Y" shape and is about 6 to 8 inches long. If the branch needs to be cut down to a smaller size, ask an adult for help.

2. Leave the branch by a heat source to dry out. Drier wood makes for a stronger frame, so let the water evaporate in a warm, dry place for several hours or even a few days.

3. While the wood is drying, cut a small rectangle out of the leather. The rectangle will be your pouch for ammo, so it should be big enough to easily wrap around your projectiles without dropping them. Make a vertical slit at one end of the leather—the slit should run parallel to the short edge of the rectangle. Do the same on the other side.

4. Next, cut two rubber bands so you have two rubber strips of equal length. At one end of the rubber strip, cut a small horizontal slit to create an opening. Do the same on the other side of that strip of rubber. Then repeat on the second rubber strip.

5. Take one end of the rubber strip and poke it through the slit on the other side. Weave it through, and you'll have made a loop. Repeat with the second rubber strip so that you have a loop on one end.

6. Slide the end of the rubber band that doesn't have the loop through one of the slits in the leather. Take the other end and push the loop you've already made through the slit in the rubber band to make another loop around the leather. Repeat this with the second rubber band on the other side of the leather.

7. Take the loop at the end of one of the rubber bands and wrap it around one of the forks of your branch. Repeat on the other side.

8. Dab some hot glue where the rubber bands grip the branch, and let the glue dry.

9. If you want to add some extra flare, wrap yarn in your favorite color around the area where the rubber bands attach to the branch. Ready to test your creation? Set up some targets, indoors or out, and see how good your aim is!

SEVEN EXTRAORDINARY ENDANGERED SPECIES

Scientists guess that there are about two million different animals spread all across the planet. There are so many types of animals (some we haven't even discovered yet!) that finding, cataloging, and understanding them all is a major field of science, called zoology, which is also where we get the word "zoo." But some of the animals out there are so rare that they're endangered. An endangered species is a species that has only a small number of its animals left and is at risk for extinction, meaning it could be totally wiped out. Many organizations work to save endangered animals by protecting their habitats and helping people learn about how rare and precious these animals are. Here are seven amazing endangered species that are beautiful, surprising, awe-inspiring, whacky, and sometimes more like us than you'd think:

1. AMUR LEOPARD

The Amur leopard is a very rare and beautifully spotted kind of leopard that lives in the farthest part of eastern Russia. This powerful cat can run up to thirty-seven miles per hour and can jump vertically ten feet into the air. That means it could jump over even the tallest adult!

2. BLACK RHINOCEROS

The black rhinoceros is a big, hulking animal with one big unicorn-like horn and one shorter horn. It's one of two species of African rhino, but unlike its neighbor the white rhino, the black rhino is a little smaller and has a hooked lip that it uses to pick and choose food from off the ground. Although the black rhino is smaller than other rhinos and a bit of a picky eater, it can grow to be over five feet tall and weigh between 1,700 and 3,100 pounds.

3. ORANGUTAN

Orangutans are big apes best known for their red and orange fur, and they can be found in the treetops of Malaysia. They use their long arms to move from branch to branch and gather lots of food. "Orangutan" is a word in the Malay language that means "forest man," and these forest men have 96.4 percent of the same genes that we do. This means that we're a very distant cousin of an orangutan!

4. SEA TURTLE

There are actually seven existing species of sea turtle, but they all share a lot in common. Sea turtles have been around for a very long time—some scientists estimate over one hundred million years! They spend most of their life in the water eating seagrass, but they come onto the beach to lay their eggs. Sea turtles never get their land legs, so they are very slow at crawling across the beach, and that's when they're most likely to be hurt or killed. Sometimes, trained volunteers will help protect the turtles while they lay their eggs, but the best thing you can do if you see one on the beach is give it plenty of space.

5. SUMATRAN ELEPHANT

The Sumatran elephant is one of the most recognizable species of elephants—think Dumbo! This five-ton elephant is found in the tropical forests of Borneo and Sumatra. The Sumatran elephant is like the giant gardener of the forest, spreading seeds wherever it goes. Right now, there are only about 2,800 of these gentle giants left, and it's critical for the health of the rainforest for these elephants to stay around and keep their garden beautiful.

6. SUNDA TIGER

The Sunda tiger used to live in the Sunda Islands, but it's now only spotted in Sumatra. It's famous for its orange fur and black stripes and has been hunted almost to extinction because of its iconic coat. To try and save this beautiful animal, people have banned tiger hunting and are trying to protect the forests that the tigers live in.

7. WESTERN LOWLAND GORILLA

Western lowland gorillas are big gorillas with dark fur, and they can stand as tall as five and a half feet when they stand upright. They can be found in western Africa, but because they live in very dense forests, no one really knows how many of them there are. They've been seen in Cameroon, Equatorial Guinea, and several other places. They tend to be slightly smaller than other types of gorillas and have brownish-gray fur and copper-colored chests.

FIVE WAYS TO BE
A CONSERVATIONIST

A lot of times, we think of the environment as something that's outside, but, really, the environment and the things it provides for us are everywhere. When we eat food that needed dirt and water to grow, ride in cars that run on gas pumped from the earth, and use water from springs and aquifers to drink and shower, we're directly interacting with our planet. And how we do those simple daily things can change the earth's health, in both good and bad ways. Because the earth is our only home, we want to preserve it and keep it as healthy as possible for us and all the plants and animals we share it with.

We can help our environment and even slow climate change, which is the gradual warming of the earth and a serious threat, by being conservationists. A conservationist is someone who tries to protect the earth, its ecosystems, and its animals by using fewer resources, like water, gas, and plastic, and choosing better-for-the-earth alternatives when we can. Conservationists are like defenders of the planet, and we need more of these heroes in the world. So if you're ready to help the earth, let's try out these five ways to be a conservationist!

1. RIDE IN THE CAR LESS

Cars, trains, and planes all use fossil fuels to get us around. Fossil fuels are buried underground and are really good at making energy, but they release a lot of gas into the air, like carbon dioxide. Too much of these gases pollute the air and make our planet too warm, which then hurts the habitats of our plants, animals, and even us. A great alternative to driving is using public transportation, like the subway or bus, because it moves more people with less fuel. If your town doesn't have a subway or bus, try carpooling with friends—it's much more fun than riding alone anyway!

2. WALK MORE, BIKE MORE

The easiest way to protect the earth is to walk or bike whenever you can! Walking only uses your human power, which is a renewable and ecofriendly source of energy. It's also a wonderful way to get some extra exercise, which can make you feel energized and happy. If you're visiting a neighborhood friend, going to the community pool, or running to a nearby store, put on some comfortable shoes, grab an adult, and hit the pavement!

3. REDUCE, REUSE, RECYCLE

You might have heard the slogan "Reduce, Reuse, Recycle" before, and it basically just means there are three main ways you can throw fewer things in the trash. Even though it's easy to use disposable products, it all ends up in a landfill, and some of it can take one hundred years or more to decompose! So, it's good to try and make less trash in the first place (that's the reduce part of things), find a new use for something instead of throwing it out (reuse), and put trash that can be made into something new into a separate bin (recycle). Next time you're about to pop something in the trash, ask yourself: Could I use less of this thing next time, use it again, or put it in recycling instead? If so, you're defending the planet with just that one tiny change!

4. FIND ALTERNATIVES TO PLASTIC

Did you know that one plastic bag takes at least five hundred years to break down? And some plastic products take even longer! That's because plastic isn't biodegradable, meaning that it can't be decomposed naturally by bacteria or other living things. Instead of using plastic bags, try switching to reusable lunch, sandwich, and snack bags; water bottles; utensils; and straws so that you can say "no" to all that plastic that ends up in landfills.

5. LET THE ELECTRICITY REST

Has anyone ever told you to turn the lights off when you leave a room? It's because they want to save some energy! The electricity that powers our lights, TVs, and household appliances uses energy from power plants. When demand is high, power plants have to work a lot, and this can be bad for the environment. Want to know a little secret for saving even more energy? If you power off a device, like a TV or computer, completely so that the red "standby" light isn't glowing, you'll save even more electricity. You can use this time away from your devices to go outside and enjoy all the pretty nature you're protecting!

CHAPTER 3:

Let's Be Athletes!

Run, jump, push, pull . . . doesn't it feel so good to see how strong you are? There's nothing better than feeling the wind in your hair and the breath huffing in your lungs as you sprint as fast as you can, pedal wildly on your bike, round the bases, or nail a jump and tough landing. Hands-on girls know that there's nothing like honing your athletic skills to make you feel great, strong, and totally powerful. And the amazing thing about being an athlete is that you can flex your muscles anywhere, anytime. With just the easiest setup and equipment—and sometimes no equipment at all—the activities in this chapter will show you how you can host a Jumping Olympics, become a Disc Bowling pro, and even fend off the bad guys with simple self-defense. So let's kick up some fun!

THE HANDS-ON GIRL'S EQUIPMENT CLOSET

You don't need a single thing (other than the right footwear!) to be an athlete—all you need is the drive to see what your body and brain can do. Many famous athletes started out by trying lots of different games and sports before finding what they loved, and it can be super fun to spice up your sporting life with new events you've never tried before. On rainy days, you can still flex your mind muscles and build your strategizing skills with dozens of brain-bending card games. And luckily, you don't need much to start dabbling in dozens of athletic endeavors.

THE PICK-UP GAME PLAY CABINET

Want to throw together a game of hopscotch or disc bowling for a sporting afternoon? Stash these simple pieces of athletic gear so you can grab-and-go your way to any game!

☐ **Sneakers**
☐ **Jump rope**
☐ **Chalk**
☐ **Flying disc**
☐ **Deck of cards**
☐ **Pencil**
☐ **Notepad**
☐ **Measuring tape**

THE TOURNAMENT-TESTED EQUIPMENT CLOSET

Inviting a few friends over for some friendly competition? Keep these sports-specific items stored away for the next time you want to tackle a team sport or build your skill in your favorite event.

- [ ] **Cones or bases**
- [ ] **Beanbags**
- [ ] **Whistle**
- [ ] **Scrimmage vests**
- [ ] **Kickball**
- [ ] **Softball**
- [ ] **Soccer ball**
- [ ] **Basketball**
- [ ] **Football**
- [ ] **Hoop**
- [ ] **Bat**
- [ ] **Flag football belt**
- [ ] **Helmet**
- [ ] **Shin guards**
- [ ] **Eye protectors**

EASY SETUP SOFTBALL

Did you know that people play softball in more than 140 countries? It's so popular because it builds teamwork, is easy to set up, and, most of all, it's super fun. If you want to knock one out of the park, all you'll need is an open space, a few supplies, and five friends to get a game going. So, collect some competitors, and get ready to play ball!

MATERIALS

- **4 cones (or any other place markers)**
- **Softball**
- **Bat**
- **Helmet for each player**
- **Glove for each player**
- **6 players or more**

SETUP

Use the four cones to mark the four points of a diamond. These cones are your bases, which are home, first, second, and third base.

Have one person stand at the center of the diamond. They're the pitcher and will throw the ball.

Have another player stand at a marker across from the pitcher (home base). They'll have the bat and be the batter.

The remaining players can spread out on the field. They'll be the base players and should stand close to a base.

SOFTBALL RULES

The pitcher must throw the ball underhand to the batter.

The batter has three chances to hit the ball. If they miss the ball, that's a strike. Once a batter has three strikes, they're out and the next player bats.

When the batter hits the ball, they'll drop the bat and run to first base. They can either stay at first base or keep running around the bases, but they're only safe when they're touching a base. Their goal is to eventually run all the way to home base without getting caught by a baseman. If a batter is caught, they're out.

The basemen will throw the ball to each other and try to tap the batter with the ball before the batter gets to a base. Basemen cannot chase a batter! If you're a baseman, try to stay close to a base so you can catch the ball and tap the batter.

Once the batter has decided to stay on a base or has been tagged out, someone else is up at bat, and the same thing is repeated. If any batter makes it all the way back to home base, they get a point!

THE JUMPING OLYMPICS

Every four years, the greatest athletes from all over the world meet in in the Olympic Games in the hopes of winning a gold, silver, or bronze medal and showing the world that they're the best competitor in their sport. These Olympians can specialize in dozens of different sports like archery, gymnastics, sailing, and even skateboarding.

One of the oldest Olympic games is the long jump. For this track-and-field event, competitors have three tries to jump as far as they can. The current world record for the most distance covered during a long jump is 29 feet and 4.36 inches, which is almost the length of a school bus. If you want to see how far you can jump, find a big grassy area and gather up some measuring tools. Once you're prepared, do a few stretches, flex your muscles, and get ready to embrace your inner Olympian!

MATERIALS

- **Large area to run and jump in (like a lawn or park)**
- **Jump rope**
- **Pencil**
- **Notepad**
- **Measuring tape**

SETUP

Find an open area with a soft surface like grass or sand to jump on to (it is *not* fun to fall on something hard like a blacktop!). Part of the area will be a runway for getting a running start and the other part will be the jumping pit. Take your jump rope and stretch it out on the ground to make a jump line, and mark where the runway ends and the jumping pit begins.

Have your pencil, notepad, and measuring tape at the sidelines to record how far you went.

RULES

Stand about six feet away from the jump line. Start running and get up to your maximum speed. When you get to the line, jump! For each game, you only get three tries to get your best distance.

SCORING

Once you land, mark the spot where you landed, or have a friend mark it for you. Then measure the distance between you and the jump line and write it down. Hint: falling will shorten your total distance, so always try to land on your feet.

After you've jumped three times, circle your longest jump. That's your new personal best record. Keep jumping and see if you can beat your record, or round up some friends and have your own Olympic long jump tournament!

HOPPED-UP HOPSCOTCH

You know those hopscotch grids painted onto the blacktop at the playground? Well, they're not the only way to play hopscotch. With just a piece of chalk, you can design your own custom hopscotch grid, full of new challenges and paths to flex your athletic abilities. There are millions of ways you can design your hopscotch court and reinvent the rules, but this is our favorite version of hopscotch with a twist!

MATERIALS
- **Blacktop or paved surface**
- **Sidewalk chalk**
- **Place marker (such as a stone)**
- **2 players or more**

INSTRUCTIONS
Use the chalk to draw a large, rectangular grid that is three squares wide and seven squares tall.

Stand at one of the short sides of the grid, then number each block beginning with 1 and ending with 21, moving left to right. The bottom right block should be 1 and the top right block should be 21. Now your court is set up!

Stand at the end of the hopscotch court that begins with 1 and turn your back so that you're facing away from the grid.

Toss your marker over your shoulder. If it lands on the court, start jumping! If not, let the next player go.

If the marker landed on the court, jump on one leg starting at 1 and follow the numbers until you get to the square your marker landed on.

Turn around on that number and jump all the way back to the starting point, following the numbers in reverse order. Try not to trip or let your other foot drop, or you'll be disqualified from that round.

If you make it all the way back to square 1, use chalk to initial the square you jumped to. That square is yours now! From now on, you are the only one who can stand on that square. Players can jump on their own initials or open squares, but they have to hop over any square that another player has marked with their initials.

Repeat steps 3 through 7 until each square has been initialed. The player with the most initialed squares wins!

GRAB A GROWN-UP!

POOL TIME PENGUIN TAG

When you imagine an athlete, what do you see? You might picture a famous dancer, or baseball player, or yourself! But what about animals? Lots of animals have to be sporty to catch their food—like penguins, which can dive 1,800 feet underwater just to find a meal. These birds are always searching for fish, krill, and squid, and they have to be awesome swimmers to catch some. Could you catch something underwater? Next time you're at a pool with a lifeguard or adult nearby, test your skill with this fishy game of pool tag! Gather up some buddies and an adult to supervise and see how athletic you would be as a penguin.

INSTRUCTIONS
The player who is "it" (the penguin) will stand at one end of the pool with their back toward the water.

The swimmers (the fish, krill, or squids) will line up in the water along the wall closest to the penguin. Each swimmer will silently choose to be a fish, squid, or krill—don't tell anyone which you choose to be!

The penguin will say, "Today, I'm looking for _____" and will say either "fish," "krill," or "squid."

If a swimmer's animal is called, she has ten seconds to start swimming to the other side of the pool. Hint: the swimmer can try to swim as quietly as possible, or the other swimmers can splash around and trick the penguin.

If the penguin hears swimming, they can turn around and dive in and try to tag the escaping fish, krill, or squid.

The penguin must tap the fish, krill, or squid before they escape to the opposite wall of the pool. If the penguin wins, the tagged swimmer becomes a penguin, but if the penguin loses, that person must go back and be the penguin again.

JUMP ROPE, FOUR WAYS

Can you imagine using a vine to jump rope? Well, that's exactly what the ancient Egyptians did when they first started skipping rope. Since then, we've found approximately a trillion ways to jump around, over, and under a swinging rope, and each one is more fun than the last. So if you've ever thought jumping rope seemed boring or too easy, try one of these jazzed-up jumps. And if you really want to have your mind blown, try searching online for jump rope competitions, which feature the elite-level jump ropers of the world and their amazing routines.

MATERIALS
• **2 jump ropes**

1. THE PINWHEEL
Have at least two (and up to six) friends stand around you in a circle. They will be the jumpers.

Hold one end of the jump rope in one hand and bend down to stretch the rope out in front of you. You'll be the spinner.

Keeping the rope low to the ground, turn in a circle so the people on the outside can jump over it. See how fast you can spin to make it harder on them to jump!

If someone gets caught on the rope, they're out.

Keep turning in a circle until only one person is left. They're the new spinner!

2. THE FIGURE EIGHT
Start jumping rope normally.

After finishing a jump, bring your right hand close to your left to swing the rope to your left side. Both of your hands should be at a 90-degree angle with your hip.

As you're doing step 2, lift your left foot so all of your weight is on your right foot.

Let the rope's momentum bring the rope up in an arc by your side and then swing the rope down to your right side. Your weight will shift in the opposite way and your hands will end up in 90-degree angles on your right side.

Keep practicing swinging back and forth until the movement is fluid and easier. It should look like you're drawing a figure eight!

Once you've mastered the swing, try jumping normally again. After making a regular jump, make a full figure eight. Try alternating between jumping normally and doing a figure eight.

3. DOUBLE DUTCH

You'll need two friends and two jump ropes for this one. Start by having two rope turners stand across from each other.

If you are a turner, take one end of one jump rope in your right hand and one end of the other jump rope in your left hand. Each turner will have one end of each rope, and the ropes will be parallel to each other.

The turners will swing one rope toward the center. As that rope starts to swing outward, swing the other rope toward the center.

Once both turners have a steady rhythm, the third person can start jumping in. Try doing different dance moves, jumps, and even rolls, and see how long you can stay in the middle.

4. THE CRISSCROSS

Start with the jump rope behind you and your hands out by your hips.

Swing the rope over your head and cross your arms at the elbows right before the rope hits the ground. This will form a loop for you to jump through!

Jump when the rope hits the ground and swing the rope up over your head.

Uncross your arms as the rope is coming back down and jump!

Keep practicing this move and alternate which arm crosses over top of the other. Pick up speed and see how fast you can go before you get tangled up!

SHARPSHOOTER BEANBAG TOSS

How good is your aim? Can you hit the same target five times in a row? Or do you want to keep sharpening your aim and have fun practicing? Whether you're a pro or beginner, a beanbag toss competition is the perfect way to work on your aim so you can be a beanbag sharpshooter. This game is perfect to play with a sibling or friend who also likes some friendly and fair competition, so find a good sport, stretch that throwing arm, and get ready to flex your tossing talent!

MATERIALS
- **Chalk**
- **Blacktop or paved surface**
- **2 to 4 players**
- **4 beanbags for each player**

SETUP
Use the chalk to draw a 4-foot by 2-foot rectangle, then walk 15 feet across the blacktop and draw another rectangle of the same size, facing the first one. (You can also use cornhole boards if you have them.)

In the top third of each rectangle, draw a circle. This will be the "hole," and it's what you'll be aiming for.

INSTRUCTIONS
Stand next to one of the rectangles, then throw a beanbag at the opposite rectangle. The front line of the rectangle you're standing at is the foul line—if you cross this, your throw doesn't count!

Each player has four beanbags and gets to throw four times in a row. Test out different ways of throwing with each beanbag. Does overhand or underhand work best?

If the bag lands in the circle, the player gets three points. If it lands in the rectangle, that's one point. If the bag doesn't land on the board or the player steps past the foul line, that's zero points.

The first player to get twenty-one points is the winner! How many three-pointers can you land in one game?

EASIEST DISC BOWLING

Bowling is so much fun, but it's not usually the sport we go for when it's a beautiful day and we want to be outside (imagine carrying a heavy bowling ball to the park!). Well, with a flying disc and a few water bottles, you can set up a bowling tournament wherever there's an open space outside. So warm up your wrists and get some friends together for a bowling competition in the air!

MATERIALS
- **10 plastic water bottles**
- **Water**
- **Flying disc**
- **Notebook**
- **Pencil or pen**

SETUP
Fill each bottle one-third of the way with water to weigh down the bottles.

Arrange the bottles in four rows to make a triangle, just like regular bowling pins would be set up. The back row will have four bottles, the next will have three, the one after that will have two, and the front will have one.

RULES

Stand thirty feet away from the pins and throw the flying disc.

Each player gets two throws during their turn to try to knock down as many pins as possible.

When a player ends their turn, count the pins they knocked down and write down their score.

Set the pins back up for the next person.

Once everyone has gone once, the round is over. After ten rounds, the game is over, and you can tally up your score to see who won. The winner gets to do their best bowling alley victory dance!

KARATE CHOPS AND TOUGH-GIRL KICKS

Imagine you're starring in your own action movie and then, all of a sudden, you're under attack! But you have some awesome hand-to-hand combat skills, so you duck and weave, throw a punch, and land a final high kick. Thanks to your training, you saved the day. And the best part? You can have those kick-butt skills in real life too by learning the basics of karate.

Karate moves are all about generating power and force in a small space, using just your own body. Have you ever seen someone break a wooden board with their bare hand? That's one of the most impressive karate moves, and it starts with practicing your strike. It takes years and years of practice to be able to break a board, but you can start your own training with some basics that even blackbelts use in their training. Here are some simple moves to get you started.

DID YOU KNOW?

Karate is a Japanese form of martial arts that began in the seventeenth century on the island of Okinawa. In those days, people weren't allowed to carry weapons, so they developed a form of defensive fighting that only requires your hands. In fact, "karate" literally means "empty hand."

STRAIGHT PUNCH (CHOKU-ZUKI)

Stand up straight in a neutral stance with your feet shoulder width apart. Bend your elbows loosely by your sides and make a fist with both hands. Your thumb should rest comfortably along the outside of your first and second fingers, and the undersides of your fists will face upward. Strike your right fist straight out from your body and rotate your wrist in so the palm of your fist faces downward by the end of the motion. To bring your arm back, rotate your wrist out so that your palm is facing up again and draw your arm back to your side. While bringing your right arm back in, strike with your left with the same technique. Practice switching between striking and pulling back until you can alternate with both arms simultaneously.

RISING BLOCK (AGE-UKE)

Begin in a neutral stance, feet shoulder width apart. Make your hands into fists at your hips with the palm side facing up. Step your right foot in to meet your left foot and bend your knees like you're about to squat. While you step into that crouch, take your right hand and start extending your fist out and upward until your arm is almost straight but still has a slight curve. As your wrist begins to pass face level, twist your wrist in so that the inside of your wrist and palm face out from your body. Stretch out the fingers of your right hand at the top of that arm movement. This is the first half of the movement, so practice this part until you can do it comfortably.

For the second part of the move, step your right foot back and slightly out to the side so you have a wide stance. Your front leg will form a 90-degree angle at the knee, and your hips will face forward. As you step back, your arms will be switching positions. Draw your right arm back down and in toward your right side. You will turn your right wrist in while lowering your hand and forming a fist. At the same time, as you start to bring your right fist down, extend your left fist out and across your body in a diagonal motion. Your arms will pass each other and form a momentary X shape in front of your chest. When they pass, your right arm should be on the inside, closest to your body, while the left will be on the outside. Once your left arm passes the right, twist the left wrist out so the palm side of the fist faces out. Your left arm's final position should be bent 45 degrees at the elbow, blocking the space in front of your forehead. At the end, return to your neutral stance. Although this one seems long, it's actually a very fast move! So, keep practicing until you can block quickly.

FRONT KICK (MAE-GERI)

Start with your right foot forward, bent at the knee, and your left foot back. Your arms should be bent at the elbows and held lightly by your sides. To start the movement, bring your left leg forward and lift it up until your thigh is parallel to the floor and perpendicular to your body. From this position, strike your foot out with your ankle bent toward your body so that the ball of your foot would make contact with the target. After the extension, bring your left foot back to its original spot using the same fluid motion. While doing this movement, your right leg should stay firmly weighted to that ground so that the left one can move quickly and lightly.

SIMPLE SELF-DEFENSE
FOR STICKY SITUATIONS

As a hands-on girl, you know how learning stuff like navigation and first aid helps you think on your feet and feel confident out in the world. And while there are lots of skills that are fun to test out and learn, self-defense is one of the skills everyone really *needs* to know. Knowing when and how to defend yourself can be critical for getting you or your friends out of a hairy situation, and it all starts with knowing when you might be in a tough spot.

HOW TO SPOT A STICKY SITUATION

BE AWARE OF YOUR SURROUNDINGS

It's really easy to get distracted and lose focus on what's going on around you, especially if we're getting a ton of texts, daydreaming about lunch, or worrying about something at school. But paying attention to where you are is the easiest and best way to stay safe. Knowing what's happening around you lets you notice if something's wrong and gives you the chance to avoid potential trouble. After all, the best way to defend yourself is to avoid having to defend yourself.

TRUST YOUR GUT

Whenever you feel like something's off or don't feel comfortable in a situation but don't know why, trust your instinct. Don't ever just ignore it, because it's always better to overreact and be a little extra cautious than to underreact. Whenever possible, move yourself out of the situation and into a place where you feel more comfortable. For example, if you get weird vibes from someone while walking down the street, step inside of a store or somewhere else with more people. Also, tell your friends or other people around you if you think something is strange. If no one is near you but you have a phone, call a parent or someone you know will answer and stay on the phone with them until you feel safe. If nobody picks up, you can pretend you're talking to someone on the phone, so anyone watching will think you have someone on the line. Just remember to stay completely aware of your surroundings, even if you're on the phone, and to look around often. Remember that letting someone else know where you are and that you're nervous in the situation is the most important thing you can do to stay safe.

KNOW WHERE TO HIT

If you have to defend yourself, you want to hit the aggressor in places that will hurt them and let you get away. The human body is very sensitive around the eyes, throat, nose, groin, and knees. Because these areas are so sensitive, you can cause a lot of damage without needing to be ridiculously strong or skilled at fighting.

GET LOUD

In a jam? Your vocal cords can be your best weapon. Scream as loudly as you can so you can scare the aggressor and get the attention of other people who can come and help. Try to scream "HELP!" so people know it's an SOS and not just a kid playing and screaming, but, really, screaming anything is better than nothing.

FIVE SIMPLE SELF-DEFENSE MOVES

1. BREAK FREE

When someone has a hold on you, the most important thing is to break their grip. Get low and turn out of their arms. Use your arms and elbows to jab and lessen their hold. Once you're free, run if you can and only fight if you have to.

2. OPEN PALM TO THE EAR

Make your hand flat and hit the other person as hard as you can on the ear with the flat of your palm. This will be very disorienting and gives you a chance to get away.

3. ELBOW STRIKE

The elbow is one of the strongest parts of your body for striking. Plant your feet, bend your arm, and jab your elbow forward like you're using it to throw a punch. You'll want to put your weight into it and aim for the face, jaw, or neck.

4. GROIN KICK

If the attacker is within kicking distance, then aim for the groin. This is also a good move if the person is close in front of you, because you can lift your knee quickly and strike the groin.

5. HEEL PALM STRIKE

Flex the wrist of your dominant hand and aim for the neck, nose, or under the jaw. Hit at an upward angle and then pull your arm back quickly (pulling back quickly will make the aggressor's head fly back and away from you).

CARD GAMES FOR SMARTIES

Did you know that in just a simple stack of playing cards, you actually have thousands of different games at your fingertips? Some challenge your speed, others test your luck, and others build your smarts. That's because when you're playing a game of cards, things are always changing, so you have to stay on your toes, watch your opponents carefully, come up with creative new strategies, and keep changing those strategies as the game changes. It's just as much of a mental workout as chess, but there are thousands of ways you can flex your brain muscles at the card table. Here are a few card games, from simple to advanced, to help you practice your scheming and strategizing skills.

SIMPLE: SPOONS

MATERIALS
- **Standard deck of cards**
- **3 players or more**
- **Spoon for each player**

GOAL
Collect four of a kind, be quick to grab a spoon, and be the last player standing.

RULES
Put all the spoons at the center of the table and take one out. Now you have one fewer spoons than players.

The dealer will shuffle the deck and then deal four cards facedown to each person.

The dealer gets one extra card, so she'll have five cards in her hand. The goal is to get four of a kind, like four hearts, diamonds, spades, or clubs, or four of a number, like four queens or eights. The dealer looks at her cards and gives the one she doesn't want to the player to her left.

The player who gets the dealer's card now has five cards. She will choose one card from her hand that she doesn't want and give it to the next player.

The last player in the rotation will put a card into a discard pile, and the dealer will take a new card from the deck.

When a player gets four of a kind, they will quickly grab a spoon.

If one person takes a spoon, everyone has to try and take one too. One player will be left without a spoon. The player who doesn't get a spoon must begin spelling the word "spoon." Each time they don't get a spoon, they must add another letter. If they get through every letter of S-P-O-O-N, they're out.

Keep playing until one person emerges the spoon victor!

INTERMEDIATE: CRAZY EIGHTS

MATERIALS
- **Standard deck of cards**
- **2 players or more**

GOAL
Get rid of all of your cards.

RULES
The dealer shuffles the deck, deals five cards facedown to each player, and places the rest of the cards in the middle of the table.

Flip the top card over. This is the starting card. If it's an eight, put it back into the pile in a random spot and flip the next card over.

Everyone should look at their cards. The player to the left of the dealer must play a card from her hand that matches the number or suit of the card on the table. So, if the face-up card is a king of diamonds, the player must play either a king or a diamond. If a player has no cards in her hand that she can play, she can draw from the deck, and she must keep drawing from the deck until she finds a card that she can play.

An eight can be played no matter what the upward-facing card is. When a player plays an eight, she gets to change the suit to anything she wants.

The first player to get rid of all of her cards wins!

ADVANCED: EGYPTIAN RAT SLAP

MATERIALS
- **Standard deck of cards**
- **2 players or more**

GOAL
Get every card.

RULES
The dealer will shuffle the deck and give cards facedown to each player until the deck is gone. No one should turn their cards over or look at them.

The player to the left of the dealer will take her top card and put it at the center of the table. If the card is a number card (not a face card or an ace), then the next player gets to put a card down.

If a player puts down an ace, jack, queen, or king, the next player also plays. Depending on the card laid down by the first player, the next player will have a certain amount of chances to put down a face card. If the first player put down a king, the next player will have three chances to get a face card. A queen gives you two chances, and a jack gives you one chance. If the next player puts down a face card during one of these chances, then the round keeps going and the following player gets to go. But if the next player puts down only number cards, then the whole pile goes to the person who played the face card and the pile winner puts another card down to start a new round.

At any point in the game, players can take the pile using a slap rule. If a slap rule is used, the first person to slap the pile wins that round and all the cards.

THE SLAP RULES
There are dozens of fun slap rules you can play in this game— choose one rule or several, or even change it up from round to round to stretch your mental acuity!

DOUBLES
Two cards of the same number are stacked on top of each other, like a six of hearts played on top of a six of diamonds.

JOKERS
Anytime a joker is played.

TENS
Two cards are played in a row and add up to ten. In this game, an ace equals one and face cards equal nine.

SANDWICH
Two cards of the same value are separated by one card of a different value, such as 2-8-2 or 9-7-9.

SLAPPING PENALTY
If a person makes a mistakes and slaps at the wrong time, they have to add two cards to the bottom of the pile.

THE TONGUE-TWISTING TOURNAMENT

Believe it or not, the tongue is one of the strongest and most flexible muscles in our bodies. It's a strong muscle too—after all, when was the last time your tongue was tired? Well, today may be the day you test the limits of your tongue's strength as you tackle these ten tongue twisters. You'll not only be flexing one of your most-used muscles (your tongue) but you'll also be building your most important muscle (your brain!) with this tournament of twisting.

So gather a few friends or family for this tournament—the more competitors, the quicker and more competitive the tongue-twisting will get.

The first person begins by saying the first sentence, which is then repeated by every other player.

In the second round, the first player repeats sentence #1 and adds sentence #2, both of which are repeated by the other players.

As you add a new sentence in each round, you have to repeat the sentences quicker and quicker, with no time for pausing. Anyone who makes a mistake or forgets a word is out.

Whoever lasts longest becomes the Tongue Twister Champion!

THE TEN TONGUE TWISTERS

1. One old ox opening oysters.
2. Two tall toucans twirling twisted turbans.
3. Three tinkering tailors totally tired.
4. Four frilly Frenchmen fanning a fainting fly.
5. Five funny farmers feeding feathered fowls.
6. Six slippery snails slid slowly seaward.
7. Seven shy soldiers shooting salted salmon.
8. Eight eccentric Englishmen exhibiting educated elephants.
9. Nine nimble noblemen nibbling nasturtiums.
10. Ten tarrying tailors toddling timidly together.

CHAPTER 4:

Let's Be Artists!

If you've had a tough day, or even if you're just feeling antsy or bored, you probably want to vent, talk, cry, hide, or just mope. We all need ways to express ourselves, whether it's to let off steam, to say what we really think, or to figure out what we're actually thinking and feeling. And making art is one of the most fun and powerful ways to express yourself. It's like venting all that pent-up energy through your hands. And the best part? There are hundreds of different art forms to choose from, like painting, writing, drawing, photography, and more. In this chapter, we'll dabble in the arts and see what stokes a creative fire in us, and we'll start by setting up in our home studio.

THE HANDS-ON GIRL'S STUDIO

When you step into an art classroom or artist's studio, you might feel inspired to dive into playing with all the art supplies, or you might be overwhelmed by how much there is and not knowing how to use it all. It's true that some types of art need very specific tools, but it's also true that you can make art with anything around you. In fact, the first artists used materials straight from the earth, like red clay and black charcoal, to make their simple cave paintings. Luckily, we have way more technology and a lot more colors, tools, and mediums available now. Whether you want to set up a starter minimalist studio or go big with an inspiration-packed maximalist space, here's what you'll need.

THE MINIMALIST STUDIO

If you want to get to art making ASAP, then this list of simple supplies will let you make hundreds of crafts, including many of the projects in this book. You probably already own most of these materials, so let's round 'em up and get our hands dirty!

- [ ] **Scissors**
- [ ] **Pencils**
- [ ] **Ruler**
- [ ] **Crayons**
- [ ] **Yarn**
- [ ] **Markers or colored pencils**
- [ ] **Paper towels and paper plates**
- [ ] **Plastic cups**
- [ ] **Liquid glue**

- [ ] **Printer paper**
- [ ] **Cardstock**
- [ ] **Phone camera**
- [ ] **Hot glue gun**
- [ ] **Ribbon**

THE MAXIMALIST STUDIO

Wanting to explore new mediums is a natural feeling for an artist. After all, the more materials you try out, the more you'll see which materials express what you're trying to say and do. So, give these options a spin if none of the above are connecting with your artistic vision.

- [ ] **Watercolor paint**
- [ ] **Watercolor paper**
- [ ] **Tempera paint**
- [ ] **Paintbrushes**
- [ ] **Craft paper**
- [ ] **Artist smock**
- [ ] **Tarp**
- [ ] **Chalk and chalkboard paint**
- [ ] **Latex gloves**
- [ ] **Silicone molds**
- [ ] **Parchment paper**

ABSTRACT PAINTING

When you think of famous artists, who do you think of? Maybe Frida Kahlo or Georgia O'Keeffe, but what about Joan Mitchell? Joan Mitchell was an abstract expressionist painter whose bright, large-format paintings often included bold brushstrokes, splatters of paint, and even finger smears. A lot of her artworks are in museums now, and they still inspire people with their chaotic and free energy.

With a few supplies, you can carry on Mitchell's artistic vision and express your own emotions through big, beautiful abstract paintings! But before you get throwing, here are some helpful color-mixing tips to get you started.

COLOR MIXING 101 FOR COLOR-SAVVY ARTISTS

MIX YOUR OWN COLORS FOR CUSTOM SECONDARY SHADES

You probably remember the color wheel from your kindergarten days—it's a wheel with slices in it like a pizza, and it has the colors red, orange, yellow, green, blue, and purple. Red, yellow, and blue are primary colors, meaning that you can't make them by mixing other colors. Orange, green, and purple are secondary colors, made by mixing the primary colors in different combinations. Red and yellow make orange, yellow and blue make green, and red and blue make purple. Because the secondary colors come from primary ones, you can mix some colors yourself instead of buying each one, and you'll get to custom craft exactly the shades of orange, yellow, and purple you'll end up with!

PAIR COMPLEMENTARY COLORS

Complementary colors are colors that sit across from each other on the color wheel, like red and green. If they are perfect complements, then they will make gray if you combine them. They also look really good together, so once you get to splattering, try pairing some complementary colors to see how they go together.

PLAY WITH CONTRAST

Try playing with contrast by painting with bright and dark colors like yellow and dark blue. Notice how they pop next to each other and make the other stand out more. Which do you like more: bright contrasts or soft complements?

MATERIALS

- **Smock**
- **Large tarp**
- **Canvas (or any other surface to paint on)**
- **Masking tape (optional)**
- **2 or more colors of tempera paint**
- **Paper plate or plastic palette**
- **Paintbrushes**

INSTRUCTIONS

1. Put on your smock, spread the tarp over your painting area, and put the canvas on the tarp.

2. If you have masking tape, use it to cover up parts of the canvas. The tape will block the paint, so you can place the tape in a fun pattern, and once the paint dries, peel it up to reveal a cool design!

3. Squeeze a bit of each paint onto your palette or plate.

4. Pause and think about how you feel. What emotions can you name that you're feeling right now? How does that make you want to paint, and what colors does it make you want to choose? Channel that emotion and energy into the painting process, and trust your gut as you pick colors and apply them however you want. If you feel like it, you can also experiment with techniques like flicking the brush or pouring paint right onto the canvas.

5. Once you feel like your art is done, step back and admire it. What word pops into your head? What do you want to title your artwork? Don't forget to also sign your art for future collectors!

NATURE PHOTOGRAPHY 101

Have you ever been wandering around outside and wished you could capture exactly what that cool-looking tree or cloud looks like? Or maybe you see a tiny flower on the ground and want to get up close and see every detail. That's the artist in you itching for some nature photography! Art is really just seeing, and every time you see something and really *notice* it, you're engaging in the appreciation of art. You can take it a step further by capturing that image and becoming an artist yourself.

That's the same impulse that drives the world's most famous nature photographers, like Cristina Mittermeier and Ansel Adams. And you too can become a nature photographer in your own backyard or street just by learning to see the world around you and snapping shots on a phone. (Remember that if you're going outside of your usual stomping grounds, let an adult know or ask them to come along.) With a smartphone, you have an entire camera and editing studio in your back pocket—much easier than hauling around a canvas and paints like artists used to have to do! But having a good camera doesn't always mean you'll be able to snap a scene exactly how you want it to look—sometimes the camera just can't see everything our eyes can see. So try these photography tips to learn how to use your camera to capture scenes that speak to you.

GOOD FOCUS, GOOD FOUNDATION

Tap the screen on the object you're really interested in so it's clear and easy to see. Bringing it into focus will emphasize it and grab attention, so always make sure your camera's focus is on the most important thing you want to capture.

CHANGE PERSPECTIVES

One reason people look at photos is because they like to see the world in a new and interesting way. When looking through your camera, test angles that you don't usually look from. Crouch, crawl, reach, and roll to get a unique perspective and see nature in a whole new way.

USE GRIDLINES

Adjust your settings so that your screen displays a three-by-three grid while you take pictures. These lines can help you compose, balance, and straighten your image. Anywhere the lines cross are important focal points, so a lot of photographers will line up the most important part of their picture where the lines cross. For an artsy look, place the most important part of the picture in the first third or last third of the screen, instead of centered. Notice how each kind of placement changes the way you experience the picture.

EMBRACE DAYLIGHT

Have you ever noticed how lamps and other lights look yellowish? That's because it's artificial light and meant for nighttime. But daylight has a better color balance and is more even and natural, and it will make your photos look closer to the way your eye sees the same thing in real life. It will also give the objects in your photo better coloring, which will automatically enhance the image.

PLAY WITH EDITING

After you capture an image, open the editing features. You can make slight adjustments, like increasing the brightness, or totally alter the photo by adding filters. The best part is that you can undo any changes you make, so go wild and experiment!

FOUR SCAVENGER HUNTS
FOR NATURE PHOTOGRAPHERS

Now that you're a picture-taking pro, let's put your skills to the test with these photo scavenger hunts.

1. SET OFF ON A BACKYARD SAFARI

Some professional photographers travel to wild places and photograph rare animals and plants for the rest of the world to see. Set out on your own adventure and document ten different plants and animals around your home. You may be surprised by the discoveries you make, and you'll have photographic evidence to share with the rest of the world after you trek back home from your safari!

2. READY FOR YOUR CLOSE-UP?

Find five common objects and get really close with your camera. You'll see a lot of details you've probably never noticed and end up with lots of abstract photos. Show your close-ups to your friends and ask them what they think it is. How many objects do you think they'll recognize?

3. IT'S A BIRD! IT'S A PLANE!

No, it's a cloud! The sky is huge and filled with floating clouds. If you look carefully, the clouds can start looking like a dog or a tree or anything else you can imagine. Point your camera upward and find three unique cloud formations. Play around with the editing tools and see what colors you can turn the clouds and what funny things you can draw over them.

4. NOW AND LATER

The world is always changing, but we usually don't notice it because it happens so slowly. But artists like photographers are trained to see little differences and to capture them for other people. Choose three places to photograph, then come back a few days or weeks later and try to take the same photo. How have things changed since the first photo?

DIY BOTANICAL BOOKMARKS

If you want to keep all the pretty flowers and leaves you spot outside alive forever, it's time to learn the art of drying plants. With a heavy book and a tiny bit of patience, you can preserve plants and use them to make one-of-a-kind designs on things like bookmarks, birthday cards, and more. They also make the perfect gift for Mom or Dad, and they'll love that it's a unique and handmade piece of art instead of something from the store. So go ahead and select some flowers, leaves, and plants that appeal to your artistic sensibility, and let's get to preserving them forever.

MATERIALS

- **Flowers, leaves, or any other plant**
- **Large book**
- **Roll of parchment paper**

- **A weight or other very heavy object, such as a stack of books**
- **Scissors**
- **Cardstock**
- **Transparent contact paper**

INSTRUCTIONS

1. Collect several of your favorite flowers, leaves, or plants, and set them aside.

2. Open the book at about the midpoint and line the two exposed pages with parchment paper.

3. Arrange the plant specimen on the parchment paper so that it lies as flat on the page as possible. If you want to dry multiple plants, make sure they don't overlap unless you want them to stick together.

4. Once all the plants are arranged, close the book and place a heavy weight or other heavy object on it. Leave the book in a dry place.

5. Check on the plants every few days until they're completely dried out.

6. Remove the dried plants carefully. Now that all the water has been dried out of them, your flowers and leaves will be very brittle and crisp, so be gentle!

7. Cut the cardstock into a 2 by 7-inch rectangle, so that it looks like a bookmark. Or you can get creative and cut your cardstock into any shape you want, as long as it's big enough to fit your dried plants.

8. Arrange your plants on the bookmark. If a stem is too long, carefully trim it with scissors.

9. Cover the bookmark with contact paper, carefully pressing it down to seal in the plants and trimming off any excess at the edges. Now you have a beautiful bouquet that will never wilt and can save your spot in a book. What other things can you decorate with your pressed plants?

HAND-LETTERING FOR HANDS-ON GIRLS

Hand-lettering is an old and beautiful art form. Since most days we type more than we handwrite, hand-lettering is usually saved for special occasions (think wedding invitations). But even though it seems fancy and hard to replicate, it's actually super easy to do yourself. With the right tools and some practice, you can incorporate pretty and trendy hand-lettering into your everyday life. You can spice up your science class outlines, or up your autograph game, or just write a fancy note to pass to a friend. The more you practice, the more you'll develop your own signature style as a hand-lettering artist.

A FEW PENMANSHIP POINTERS BEFORE YOU START

With hand-lettering, you can use any writing tool or paper you like, but remember that each supply will create a different final artwork. So try out a bunch of different materials to find which one feels most like you.

Did you know that hand-lettering and calligraphy are not the same? Calligraphy is about writing in one fluid movement, with all letters connecting, but hand-lettering is about carefully designing letters with a particular aesthetic. It's almost like designing your own font! The main difference is that you can sketch your design for hand-lettering first and then fill it in.

Try to sit up straight while writing. It might not seem like it would matter, but good physical form will carry over to your letters.

MATERIALS

- **Ruler**
- **Pencil**
- **8.5 by 11-inch printer paper**
- **Eraser**

INSTRUCTIONS

1. Choose a word to write, like your name or a favorite word. You'll be writing it over and over, so choose something that makes you smile.

2. Use a ruler and a pencil to draw four evenly spaced parallel lines on the paper. The top line is called the ascender, the next line is the x height, the next is the base, and the bottom line is the descender. Each line represents a point that different letters will hit.

3. Beginning at the baseline, try writing your word in standard cursive. Lowercase letters will fit between the base and the x height, stems will fall between the base and descender (stems are the bottom part of letters like "y"), and the tops of tall letters will go between x height and ascender (like the tall line of "h").

4. Next, write the word in cursive again, but push down to create a thick line on the downstrokes. You've just changed the text weight, and "weight" is how we measure the thickness of a line. When you make a font on the computer bold and it makes the letters thicker, you're changing the weight of that font. Notice how the thicker lines of your hand-lettered word give the text weight variation.

5. For letters with stems (g, y, etc.), try adding a loop that continues the letter toward the right, connecting it to the next letter.

6. For letters that you cross or dot (t, f, i, etc.), try adding style to the mark, like lengthening the line you use to cross a "t" or dotting your "i" with a heart or peace symbol.

Hand-lettering is all about practice and experimentation, so keep writing and trying out different styles. Try looking up other artists online and imitating their styles to hone your skill. As you learn what flourishes you like, you can then riff on them in your own custom lettering.

FIVE POEMS TO RECITE OUTSIDE

Have you ever been outside, looking at the sky, feeling the wind, wishing you had words to describe it all? Nature is one of the most powerful forces that stirs our souls, and for thousands of years it's been a muse for poets, who have all tried to grasp and lyricize the experience of being outside. Now you can also step into what nature was like for them by reading their words, sometimes written a hundred years ago. What parts of nature are the same? What's different about the way they describe it? How would you describe that same thing?

Check out the poems below (or find your own at poetry. org!) and recite your favorite one outside, giving your best performance for the trees and sky with all you've got. Or, if you want to step into a poet's shoes, grab a pad and scribble your own poem. It doesn't matter how long or short it is—all you have to do is look carefully at what's around you, and the inspiration will come. After all, a flash of inspiration is where all poetry begins!

1. "A JELLY-FISH"

Marianne Moore

1887–1972

Marianne Moore was an American poet who was part of the modernist movement. This movement broke away from traditional forms and rules and embraced experimentation and free thinking. She was a transformational figure in American poetry and became one of the first celebrity poets in the country, winning the National Book Award, Pulitzer Prize, and the National Medal for Literature.

Visible, invisible,

A fluctuating charm,

An amber-colored amethyst

Inhabits it; your arm

Approaches, and

It opens and

It closes;

You have meant

To catch it,

And it shrivels;

You abandon

Your intent—

It opens, and it

Closes and you

Reach for it—

The blue

Surrounding it

Grows cloudy, and

It floats away

From you.

2. "WHO HAS SEEN THE WIND?"

Christina Rossetti

1830–1894

Christina Rossetti was an English poet most known for her romantic, religious, and children's poems. She was a master of prosody, which is a pattern of rhythm and sound in poetry, and her work strongly influenced many famous writers, such as Virginia Woolf and Elizabeth Jennings.

Who has seen the wind?

Neither I nor you.

But when the leaves hang trembling,

The wind is passing through.

Who has seen the wind?

Neither you nor I.

But when the trees bow down their heads,

The wind is passing by.

3. "MONADNOCK IN EARLY SPRING"

Amy Lowell

1874–1925

Amy Lowell was an American poet of the imagism movement. The imagism movement championed writing that was filled with detailed, precise imagery and clear language. She published over a dozen books, was a fierce advocate for and publisher of her fellow poets, and won a Pulitzer Prize for Poetry in 1926, after her death.

Cloud-topped and splendid, dominating all

   The little lesser hills which compass thee,

   Thou standest, bright with April's buoyancy,

Yet holding Winter in some shaded wall

Of stern, steep rock; and startled by the call

   Of Spring, thy trees flush with expectancy

   And cast a cloud of crimson, silently,

Above thy snowy crevices where fall

   Pale shrivelled oak leaves, while the snow beneath

   Melts at their phantom touch. Another year

Is quick with import. Such each year has been.

   Unmoved thou watchest all, and all bequeath

   Some jewel to thy diadem of power,

Thou pledge of greater majesty unseen.

4. "CLOUDS"

Anonymous

Sometimes the author of a poem, book, or other creative work wants to remain anonymous, like the author of this poem, "Clouds." Artists can hide their identity by using a made-up name, which is called a pen name, a pseudonym, or a nom de plume. There are lots of reasons why a creator might want to remain unnamed, but we owe many of our masterpieces to mysterious anonymous artists.

White sheep, white sheep,

On a blue hill,

When the wind stops,

You all stand still.

When the wind blows,

You walk away slow.

White sheep, white sheep,

Where do you go?

5. "A GRAIN OF SAND"

Frances Ellen Watkins Harper
1825–1911

Frances Ellen Watkins Harper was an abolitionist, suffragist, poet, and public speaker. She published her first book of poetry at the age of twenty and was one of the first African-American women to be published in the United States.

Do you see this grain of sand

Lying loosely in my hand?

Do you know to me it brought

Just a simple loving thought?

When one gazes night by night

On the glorious stars of light,

Oh how little seems the span

Measured round the life of man.

Oh! how fleeting are his years

With their smiles and their tears;

Can it be that God does care

For such atoms as we are?

Then outspake this grain of sand

"I was fashioned by His hand

In the star lit realms of space

I was made to have a place."

Should the ocean flood the world,

Were its mountains 'gainst me hurled

All the force they could employ

Wouldn't a single grain destroy;

And if I, a thing so light,

Have a place within His sight;

You are linked unto his throne

Cannot live nor die alone.

WATERCOLOR PAINTING WORKSHOP

Watercolor painting is one of the oldest art forms, and it was used as far back as ancient Egypt to decorate manuscripts with illustrations. It's just as popular today as it was then—in fact, the book you're holding right now has hand-painted watercolor art! Watercolor has had such lasting power because it's not only pretty but also easy to do, and it's crazy fun to play around with and mix all the colors. All you really need is watercolor paper, a watercolor palette, a brush, and your artistic vision, and you'll have hours of fun sketching and painting everything around you.

MATERIALS

- **Small or medium brush with soft, usually synthetic bristles**
- **Jar or cup of water**
- **Tray or palette of assorted watercolor paints in cake (dry) form**
- **Pencil**
- **Pack of watercolor paper**
- **Roll of paper towels**
- **White crayon (optional)**

INSTRUCTIONS

1. Dip your brush into the water and wet each watercolor cake. Water activates the paint, so add a lot! Let the water sit until the paint becomes fluid.

2. While the cakes are softening, use a pencil to make a light outline of what you want to paint on the watercolor paper. Watercolor is easy to see through, so make sure your drawing is very light so that the lines don't stand out once you start painting.

3. Once the paint is liquid and you have your pencil sketch, decide what colors you want to paint each part of your picture. Start with your lightest colors first, like yellow, and dip your brush into the paint and brush it on where you want it. Continue with any other colors you want, always filling in the lightest colors first and ending with the darkest colors, which can help keep your painting from getting too dark and murky.

4. When you want to change colors, just rinse your brush in your cup of water and dab the excess water on a paper towel. Helpful hint: watercolor is about layering, so when you change colors, try letting one layer of color dry and then going back to add another! Experiment with how the colors and effects change when you layer the colors.

NEED A FEW IDEAS TO GET PAINTING? TRY THESE!

PRETTY POPPIES

Artists love painting flowers with watercolor paint because they come out so bright and beautifully. Bright-red poppies are super fun to paint, especially when you simplify them. All you have to do is make a cluster of large red blobs and dab a little black at the center of each. Then add some long, thin stems, and bam—you have a pretty little bundle of poppies. If you want to add more flowers to your watercolor bouquet, use the same technique in different colors to add violets, carnations, and more.

THE HIDDEN MESSAGE

Did you know you can hide secret messages in your watercolors? If you draw on watercolor paper with a white crayon and then start painting, the paint will stain everything but the wax-covered areas. Try using your white crayon on the white paper to create a hidden message or picture, then give it to a friend and let them paint on some watercolors to reveal your surprise.

A STARRY GALAXY

Just like Van Gogh and his famous *The Starry Night* painting, you can paint your own airy galaxy of stars using your watercolors. Take your pencil and lightly sketch tiny circles all over your watercolor paper. These are your stars. Then, without covering the circles, quickly paint a layer of water (no colors) all over the page. While the page is wet, start dabbing purple, blue, and black on the wet parts, brushing it slightly so it blends. The paint will spread out and mix together on the wet surface but go around the dry areas. Keep adding your night-sky colors until those white, dry circles transform into twinkling stars. If you want to make even more stars or brighten up your stars, add a layer of white craft paint after the watercolors have dried for an extra-starry galaxy.

DIY NAME GARLAND

Do you ever wish you had something fun and handmade to add to your room that just screams *you*? Well, a DIY name garland is the you-est thing there is! With just a few minutes and a few simple crafting supplies, you can make a cute and customized garland spelling out your name—it's perfect to hang over your bed, in your locker, or anywhere else you need more style and flair.

MATERIALS

- **Gradient paint strip samples from the hardware store**
- **Scissors**
- **Ruler**
- **Construction paper, cardstock, or thin cardboard**
- **Bottle of glue**
- **Roll of ribbon**
- **Pencil**
- **Hot glue gun**

INSTRUCTIONS

1. Choose your favorite colors from the paint sample strips. Cut the paint chips into 1-inch strips and then arrange them into the shapes of the letters of your name. Glue each letter to your construction paper, cardboard, or other sturdy backing, then cut out each letter.

2. Once your letters are ready to go, line them up in order and then flip them over so the back side of the letters are facing up (your name and the letters will both be backward).

3. Unspool some ribbon and lay it on top of the letters to make sure you like the letter spacing on the ribbon and have enough ribbon on each end to hang the garland. Once you've checked the length of the ribbon, cut it to the size you need.

4. Use a hot glue gun to glue the ribbon onto the back of each letter.

5. After the glue cools and hardens, your garland is ready to hang up! Remember your name garland is representing you, so spice it up and personalize it as much as you want—try adding extra ribbons, gluing on pompoms, or adding a coat of glitter paint!

MAKE YOUR OWN CHALKBOARD

When you hear the word "chalkboard," what do you think of? Probably a long, flat blackboard nailed to the wall in some old-fashioned classroom, right? Well, think again! With chalkboard paint, almost anything can become a surface to decorate and customize. And chalk is a super-fun medium to get artistic with, since it draws and colors in so differently compared with markers. Go on a hunt for a few uncommon objects, like a unique stone from outside or an old jar from a thrift store, then add a couple of layers of chalkboard paint. Now you can have a blank black canvas to decorate with awesome designs, your favorite quotes, that lyric that's stuck in your head, or whatever feels fun to you!

MATERIALS

- **Latex or latex alternative gloves**
- **2-ounce bottle of chalkboard paint**
- **Plastic disposable plate**
- **Foam paintbrush**
- **Pack of chalk or chalkboard markers**

INSTRUCTIONS

1. Clean the surface of your object. If you want to make a perfectly square or rectangular chalkboard surface, use tape to block off your shape. Or if you want to make sure you don't get paint on any part of your object, tape it off to protect it.

2. Put on a pair of gloves and pour some chalkboard paint onto the plastic plate.

3. Apply the paint with a foam brush. Let the paint dry and then add another layer so the paint is opaque. Peel any tape off.

4. Once the paint is dry,
   grab your chalk and get to
   decorating!

NEED INSPIRATION? TRY THESE IDEAS!

Collect five to ten rocks, cover them in chalkboard paint, then write one word of a secret message on each of the rocks. Hide them around the house or yard, then challenge your siblings or friends to find all the rocks to spell out the hidden message.

Give old or thrift store placemats a bold makeover by painting their surface with chalkboard paint. Then have fun writing your name on your own placemat and doodling on it as you eat!

Ask your adult if you can paint a small section of a bedroom wall with chalkboard paint to use as a bulletin board. You can hang an empty frame on it to make it look extra cute, or just decorate it with doodles, reminders, lyrics, and anything else you want to use to jazz up your bedroom decor!

MELTED CRAYON SAMURAI STARS

Long ago, Japan had powerful military leaders called samurai who defended their people with honor and special tools, like the shuriken. A shuriken is a star-shaped disc that samurai could throw—it was like a supersharp flying disc! Of course, real shurikens are tools and not toys, but you can make your own version with a few leftover crayons and a star-shaped mold. With these stars in hand, you can show off your might *and* draw an awesome picture!

MATERIALS
- **Oven**
- **Package of crayons**
- **Tray of star-shaped silicone molds**

INSTRUCTIONS

1. Have an adult preheat the oven to 220°F.

2. Peel the paper label off the crayons and break them into small pieces that will fit inside the silicone mold. Mix up your colors if you want tie-dyed stars!

3. Have an adult place the molds into the oven, bake until the crayons are completely melted into a liquid (15 to 20 minutes), and remove the tray and set on the counter to cool.

4. Once the crayon wax has cooled, it will become hard again!

5. Once the stars have solidified, gently push them out of the mold. Now your samurai stars are ready for action! Take them outside to practice your samurai star-throwing skills, or use their drawing powers to sketch yourself as a powerful samurai leader!

THREE TREASURE HUNTS FOR THE LIBRARY

Rainy days are made for a trip to the library, where you can pile up a stack of books to take home, then curl up on the couch for a reading day. But because there are so many books at the library, sometimes it can feel overwhelming to find something you really love. And sometimes what you think you love is totally different from what you actually end up loving. That's why it's fun to try new genres you've never read before—and hey, if you don't like a new book, you can always just return it to the library! So let's embark on a quest to unearth as many hidden gems as possible. All you'll need is a pencil and a copy of these three library treasure hunts for each player.

1. AWARD-WINNING BOOKS

☐ Locate *A WRINKLE IN TIME* by Madeleine L'Engle, read the author bio, and write down three facts about Madeleine's life.

☐ *NEW KID* by Jerry Craft was the first graphic novel to ever win the Newbery Medal. Track a copy down and check its publication date.

☐ Collect three books with **A MEDAL ON THE COVER**. Choose at least one of them to check out and read.

☐ Find **KATE DICAMILLO**'s famous novel about a scruffy dog. Hint: This dog shares its name with a grocery store chain!

☐ Jasmine Warga's novel, *OTHER WORDS FOR HOME*, tells the story of a girl moving to the U.S. from a distant country. After tracking down this novel, find the library's world atlas and see where the girl's from and where she's going.

2. AWESOME GROWN-UP GIRLS

☐ *ELEANOR ROOSEVELT: A LIFE OF DISCOVERY* is a biography written by Russell Freedman that recounts the life of a strong first lady of the U.S. Look through the book and find two important projects she contributed to.

☐ *CLAUDETTE COLVIN: TWICE TOWARD JUSTICE* by Phillip Hoose is a book for ambitious readers, so read the first few pages and look up any words you don't know in the dictionary.

☐ Amy Ephron's *THE CASTLE IN THE MIST* follows the adventures of Tess and her brother, Max, but what kind of adventures will they have? Once you've uncovered this book, find another book of the same genre.

☐ **FIND TWO BOOKS** (fiction or nonfiction) that have a female main character and were written by a female writer.

☐ This book by **MARGOT LEE SHETTERLY** details the real-life struggles and accomplishments of four female mathematicians who helped NASA and its space program. In what section of the library might you find it? See if you can spot it.

3. MORE THAN JUST BOOKS

☐ Try finding *CALVIN AND HOBBES* and then see what other comics or graphic novels your library has.

☐ Locate the poetry section. Then look for books by a poet named **NAOMI SHIHAB NYE** or **JACQUELINE WOODSON**.

☐ Find the librarian and **INTRODUCE YOURSELF**. While you're there, ask the librarian what books have been most popular lately for readers your age.

☐ Plays are amazing to see in person, but they're great to read too. Find the library's drama section and **FIND A PLAY** that has multiple copies on the bookshelf.

☐ An anthology is a collection of short stories, poems, and other types of writing, and it's a fantastic way to discover new writers that you'll like! **FIND AN ANTHOLOGY** and pick out a writer that impresses you.

THE HANDS-ON GIRL'S READING LIST

Here's a secret for surviving bad days: Hide in a book. No matter how crummy the day was, how annoying everyone is being, and how plain old cranky you are, you can step through the magic portal of a book and escape it all. Inside a book, there's a whole different world, where you don't have to be you and you don't have to live where you live and you definitely don't need to put up with all the unfair things that are bothering you. Instead, you can be a spy named Harriet who's cataloging in her notebook what everyone is *really* up to. Or you can be Claudia Kincaid, who runs away from home and camps out in an art museum.

In book world, there are no rules, no responsibilities, definitely no homework, and you can be anything you want to be, from a spy to an astronaut to a fairy. So pile up a few of these books, both current and classic, and keep them at the ready for anytime you need an escape or even just a new adventure.

CLASSICS

Harriet the Spy
Louise Fitzhugh

Little Women
Louisa May Alcott

The Penderwicks
Jeanne Birdsall

Tuesdays at the Castle
Jessica Day George

The House on Mango Street
Sandra Cisneros

The Westing Game
Ellen Raskin

Matilda
Roald Dahl

From the Mixed-Up Files of Mrs. Basil E. Frankweiler
E. L. Konigsburg

Pippi Longstocking
Astrid Lindgren

Ella Enchanted
Gail Carson Levine

Anne of Green Gables
L. M. Montgomery

A Wrinkle in Time
Madeleine L'Engle

Roll of Thunder, Hear My Cry
Mildred D. Taylor

NEW FAVORITES

The Girl Who Drank the Moon
Kelly Barnhill

The Prince and the Dressmaker
by Jen Wang

Awkward
Svetlana Chmakova

York: The Shadow Cipher
Laura Ruby

Ava and Pip
Carol Weston

Song for a Whale
Lynne Kelly

A Dash of Trouble
Anna Meriano

Brown Girl Dreaming
Jacqueline Woodson

Etiquette & Espionage
Gail Carriger

Book Scavenger
Jennifer Chambliss Bertman

Counting by 7s
Holly Goldberg Sloan

Women in Science: 50 Fearless Pioneers Who Changed the World
Rachel Ignotofsky

The Thing About Luck
Cynthia Kadohata

CHAPTER 5:

Let's Be
Builders!

Just like hands-on girls, builders use their brains and brawn in creative ways to beautify and better the things around them. While drilling, sanding, and measuring their way through each project, builders are constantly solving problems, inventing new ways of doing things, and testing different ideas. And just like with anyone who knows a lot about one subject, builders all started by mastering the basics and then taking little steps to learn more with each new build. From crafting a bench to building a house, every building project relies on many of the same fundamental skills, like measuring, hammering, sanding, and painting. So, grab your toolbox and let's jump-start your journey to becoming a master builder.

THE HANDS-ON GIRL'S TOOLBOX

Tools are one of the big things that separates us as humans from most animals—you don't usually see a deer using a ladder to get the top leaves off a tree, right? But we've been using tools to make our lives easier for thousands of years. Since the Stone Age, people have been inventing and reinventing tools to be stronger and more efficient (just look up some stone tools to see how far we've come). There are hundreds of tools to choose from these days, but you can take on most projects with a simple set of just a few of them. And if you already have the essentials and want an upgrade, we'll cover that too!

THE APPRENTICE TOOLBOX

Feeling a little overwhelmed by all the options at the hardware store? You don't need most of that stuff—don't worry. With this list, you can put together a basic set of tools that will help you get through most projects.

- ☐ **Work Gloves**
- ☐ **Pencil**
- ☐ **Measuring tape**
- ☐ **Scissors**
- ☐ **Masking tape or duct tape**
- ☐ **Hammer**
- ☐ **Nails**
- ☐ **Phillips-head screwdriver with interchangeable heads**
- ☐ **Flat-head screwdriver**

- [ ] **Screws**
- [ ] **Sandpaper**
- [ ] **Paint or stain**
- [ ] **Brushes**
- [ ] **Level**
- [ ] **Saw**

THE MASTER TOOLBOX

When you want to push your building prowess to the next level, try adding some of these items to your kit. But remember—adding more tools doesn't always make a project easier, so only get more tools if you really need them.

- [ ] **Toolbelt**
- [ ] **Chalk line**
- [ ] **Pliers**
- [ ] **Crescent wrench**
- [ ] **Hex key set**
- [ ] **Power sander**
- [ ] **Power drill with bits**
- [ ] **Clothesline or rope**
- [ ] **Tarp**

HANDS-ON ACTIVITY

THE EASIEST TREE SWING

What do trapeze artists, wrecking balls, and swings all have in common? They have pendulum movement! This kind of movement is unique because it constantly goes back and forth between kinetic and potential energy, and this switching creates a steady swing. Want to test out the physics for yourself? Creating a pendulum is easier than you might think. In fact, you can build a DIY swing and have your own giant pendulum in about an hour! So, grab an adult and some supplies, and let's prove the power of the pendulum!

MATERIALS

- 1 (2 by 12 by 22-inch) wood board
- Drill with 11/16-inch bit
- Sandpaper
- Tape measure
- Braided rope (at least 36 feet long, depending on height of branch)
- Masking tape
- Marker

INSTRUCTIONS

1. If you're starting with a larger 2 by 12-inch board, such as a standard 2 by 12 by 96-inch board, have an adult cut it down to 22 inches in length. (Save the scrap for another swing or project!) Now you'll have a rectangle that is 12 inches wide and 22 inches long.

2. Using a 11/16-inch drill bit, drill a hole at each corner, leaving 1 to 2 inches of space between the hole and the sides of the board.

3. Sand the surface and edges of the board. No one wants a splinter, so sand until each side is smooth (see page 135)!

4. The length of rope you need will depend on the tree branch you choose, so pick out a sturdy branch at least 7 feet from the ground. Throw the rope over the tree branch twice so that it creates a loop around the branch and hangs down on both sides.

5. Cut the rope so that the ends just touch the ground.

6. Repeat steps 4 and 5 on the same branch about 20 inches away from the first rope.

7. Wrap tape around both ends of each rope. This keeps the rope from fraying.

8. Make a mark on each rope where you want the board to be suspended. The board should be high enough that you can sit and swing your legs comfortably.

9. Take each taped rope end and thread it through one of the board's four holes.

10. Tie a strong knot, like an overhand knot (see page 53) under each corner of the board. Use the mark you made earlier to help guide you on how high from the ground to place the knot.

11. Test out your swing. If it's level and the height's perfect, tie one or two more knots under the first ones to ensure maximum hold. Now you're ready to switch between kinetic and potential energy all day long!

HOW TO CHANGE A BIKE TIRE

With a sturdy set of wheels, you're virtually unstoppable . . . well, at least until you get a tire puncture! If you've never changed a bike tire, it can seem a little daunting at first. But just like with any project, when we break it down, it's actually pretty easy.

First, let's figure out if you even need to change the tire or if you can just patch it up. The tire can be repaired with a repair kit if the puncture checks these three boxes:

☐ You can find the damaged area quickly and there's no noticeable air loss.

☐ The hole is in the tread. If instead the puncture is on the edge of the tread or the side of the tire, then you'll need a replacement.

☐ The damage isn't wider than ¼ inch.

If you can't repair the tire, then it's time to replace it! Just follow the instructions below, and you'll be back on the road in no time.

DID YOU KNOW?
Did you know that the first bicycles ever invented used wheels that were just metal hoops on wooden spokes (talk about a bumpy ride!)? Since then we've upgraded to much smoother rubber tires. They can carry us for thousands of miles. In fact, the biking world record holder rode over 15,744 miles in one journey across India.

MATERIALS

- **Wrench**
- **2 bike tire levers**
- **Bike tire**
- **Bike tube**
- **Bike tire pump**

INSTRUCTIONS

1. Take off the wheel. Some bikes have a quick release lever and others may require a wrench.

2. Unscrew or uncap the tire valve to deflate the old tire.

3. Insert the bike lever between the rubber tire and the metal wheel rim. The lever should be over the rubber part of the wheel.

4. Hook the lever to pull the tire from the rim. Now the lever should be over the metal part of the wheel. Leave this lever here for now.

5. Use the second bike lever to go around the rest of the wheel and gently pull the tire out of the rim.

6. Take out the inner tube.

7. Inspect the tire. If the treads are worn or there's a hole that can't be patched easily, replace the tire as well as the tube.

8. Put the new tire around the wheel rim. One side of the tire should be in the rim and the other should be left open (you'll put the tube in through the open side). Make sure the tread is facing the same direction as the wheel, so if the wheel is spinning to the right, then the tread should also point toward the right.

9. Attach the pump to the air valve on the new tube and pump it up a little so that it becomes round but not fully inflated.

10. Put the valve through the rim. This part of the tube should now be sandwiched between the wheel rim and the tire.

11. Bring the tire over the tube and work the rest of the tube in between the tire and the rim.

12. Starting at the valve, push the open side of the tire inside the rim. Go around the entire tire and be careful not to pinch the tube!

13. Check to see if the seam of the tire is even around the entire wheel on both sides. If it is, then the tire is seated correctly!

14. Inflate the tire. Helpful hint: the side of each tire will be labeled with its ideal pressure. Look for that psi number and pump up the tire until the gauge on your pump gets close to that number.

15. Tighten or cap the valve.

16. Fasten the wheel back onto your bike. Now your bike is as good as new, and you're ready to train for your own biking world record!

SMART SANDING AND HOW TO DO IT

If you love to build things, you'll run into something you have to sand soon enough, whether you're smoothing out the boards for a bench or sanding the paint off a table for your next color makeover. Sanding is important for lots of reasons:

1. It gets rid of splinters.
2. It makes wood much smoother, so it looks nicer and feels better.
3. It removes marks or scratches.
4. It helps prepare wood for staining or painting.
5. It lets you create rounded edges and other cool features in wood.

Sanding, like most woodworking and building, really only comes down to using a few simple tools, knowing the basics, and then getting after it with all your energy.

WHAT TYPE OF SANDPAPER SHOULD YOU USE?

Before you jump in and start sanding that annoying splinter you just spotted in your wood, it'll be easier if you understand what types of sandpaper and tools you can use. Sandpaper comes in various levels of grit, from really fine, smooth sandpaper to very coarse, harsh sandpaper. The coarser the grit on your sandpaper, the more friction it will create when rubbed over wood. Coarse sandpaper, which usually starts at a 40 or 60 grit, is perfect for when you start sanding a really rough piece of wood that's never been sanded before. The coarse grit will sand off splinters, nicks, or scratches in the wood. For pieces of wood that are already smooth—or if you've already rubbed them with rough sandpaper for a while—you'll want to choose a smoother-grit sandpaper, with a 100 to 200 grit. You can even find superfine finishing sandpaper (as high as 300 grit) that will really smooth out and put the final touches on a piece of wood or prepare it for painting or staining. Just make sure you wipe the wood with a damp cloth and let it dry before painting, or you'll be painting on top of a fine layer of sawdust.

SELECT YOUR SANDING TOOLS

Next, you want to think about what tools you'll want to use to sand. The easiest—and most common—are your own hands. You can hold the sandpaper on the non-sanding, smooth side and rub the gritty side over the wood. Another option is to buy a sanding block, which is basically a flat surface with a handle that holds your sandpaper for you, so you can spare your hands and get a better grip on the sandpaper. Next to the sanding blocks at the hardware store, you might also spot sanding sponges, which are exactly what they sound like: sponges, but with gritty sandpaper exteriors instead of soft, porous exteriors. And the final option for sanding, if you and your grown-up want to rev up a power tool, is an electric sander, which will do most of the work for you and is great for big projects where sanding by hand could take forever.

PREP AND SAND AWAY

Once you know what type of sandpaper and what sanding tools you want to use, you're ready to get started. Before sanding, it's always a good idea to clean the wood with a damp rag and then let it dry. A mask that covers your nose and mouth can be helpful here too, for the sawdust sanding will kick up. There isn't one right way to sand once you get started, so you can try all different ways to see what works best for you. One way to do it is to just rub your sandpaper back and forth in a straight line along the grain. This works great if there's a mark or scratch in the wood you want to sand away. Another option is to make a small, circular motion with your sandpaper, starting in one section of your wood and then gradually moving to other sections. This circular motion can help create a smooth, uniform surface on your wood, which is what you want anytime you're staining or painting a piece.

Remember: Sanding takes patience, and it's a dusty job, but it'll be worth it once you see your gleaming, smooth, awesome-looking piece that you built yourself.

THE BASICS OF PAINTING

Do you sometimes look around your room and wish it looked cuter or even just *different*? Do you have an old bookshelf or nightstand that's scratched and faded? Do you sometimes wish your favorite desk was purple instead of green? Well, once you learn the basics of painting, you can transform a boring room or piece of furniture into something pretty, colorful, and totally you. And you'll be so surprised how a fresh coat of paint can be exactly the high impact makeover you've been craving. With just a few basics tucked under your painter's belt, you'll be ready to stir up a whole new storm of color in your room and house.

SET YOURSELF UP FOR SUCCESS

It is super tempting to start by painting a wall or a room so you get a big impact right away, but you'll actually enjoy painting a lot more if you practice on smaller things, like a bookshelf or table, while you get the hang of it. (If you're painting furniture, just make sure you prepare the wood by sanding it and wiping it off first, and check out Smart Sanding and How to Do It on page 135 for more tips.) The most important rule with painting is to set yourself up for success by prepping properly. That sounds like a cliché, but you'll thank yourself a thousand times over if you don't have to run all over the house in your paint-splattered clothes to get things you forgot about!

You'll want to start by thinking about what spot inside or outside would be a good place to paint. If there's going to be nice weather for the next few days, painting outside can make things way easier since you don't have worry as much about paint splattering on the floor or in the wrong place. But remember that paint can take several hours to dry, so you also want to check that the weather forecast doesn't call for rain. You can paint inside too as long as you protect your surfaces by placing whatever you are painting on top of newspaper, cardboard, or a tarp before you start. Because if there's one rule about painting, it's that it can definitely get messy—which, after all, is what makes it so fun.

SELECTING THE PERFECT PAINT AND BRUSH

Once you have a good place to paint, you'll next need to decide what type of paint to use. We all know paint comes in every color of the rainbow, but it also can have different finishes. One option is glossy paint, which means the paint has a shine to it once it dries. The opposite of glossy paint is called flat paint, which is matte and has no shine at all. And in the middle are finishes like satin or semi-gloss, which have more or less shine to them. Painters tend to prefer paint that is less shiny, like eggshell or satin, for walls, while glossier finishes are better for furniture.

The way to think about it is that glossy paint works best for things that might get dirty or receive more use, because the shiny finish is easier to wipe clean. And the last thing to consider is whether you want to use water-based (also called latex) or oil-based paint. Water-based paint is easier to work with since it can be cleaned up with a just bit of water, so it's a perfect place to start if you want easy cleanup on your first project.

After you choose your paint, make sure you have the right type of paintbrush for your project. Paintbrushes can be made of different types of materials, and they can be super wide or super narrow and everything in between. Wider ones are better for painting large surfaces like a tabletop, while narrower brushes are good for painting smaller things like the edge of a bookshelf.

If you're painting with a few different colors, it'll be much easier for you to have a separate brush for each color—and if that's not doable, then at least make sure you clean the brush really well before using it with a new color.

THE BEST PAINTING TECHNIQUES

You've got your brush; you've got your paint; now you can start painting. Most of the time, it works best to paint *with* the grain of the wood. This just means that whatever direction the lines on the wood (also called the grain) are running, you should paint in that same direction too. Painting with the grain makes the paint go on smoother and look nicer. But if you're looking for your piece to have a rough, cool-looking texture, you might throw that advice out the window and paint against the grain to see how it looks. You can even try both techniques on the back of a piece, if you just want to see how they look.

One thing that's easy to forget about painting is that you almost always need two or three coats. Most paints will only reach their true color—the one you picked out from the sample—after they're thoroughly layered in a few coats. The can of paint will tell you exactly when you can recoat and how much dry time you'll need in between. But, hey, if you love the softer look of your paint after just one coat, then stick with that—you're the painter in charge here!

After you're done, it's time to clean up. But it won't be so bad if you prepped your space carefully before you got started. If you decided to paint outside, all you have to do is clean your brushes and close up your paint can. If you're inside, you'll also throw away the newspaper or cardboard you painted on top of. Cleaning paintbrushes is pretty easy too. You can just wash out water-based paint by running warm water over your brush and rubbing it with your hands until no more color flows out of it. Place your brushes in a spot where they can dry fully so they're ready to grab for your next project. Once cleanup is done, it's time to sit back, relax, and admire your work . . . and maybe even start daydreaming about the next project!

FIVE WAYS TO REPURPOSE FOUND WOOD

When you run across a fallen branch in the park or yard, or a log in the woods, what do you do? Most people just ignore it, or maybe kick at it a little to see what's underneath. But wood is a lot more interesting than that. You can use wood you find lying around to build things, play games, or even make tools. And you don't have to be a fancy woodworker to do it. In fact, you can often repurpose wood into all types of cool things using just your own two hands. The next time you find some branches lying in the grass, try these ideas:

1. BUILD A STICK HUT

If you find longer branches or sticks—from four to six feet long—you can use them to build a triangular hut or fort. Take the sticks and lean them against each other to form a triangle or pyramid shape, making sure to leave one spot without sticks as your door. Keep adding as many branches as you can find to make your hut extra sturdy.

2. TRANSFORM IT INTO A SOFTBALL BAT

A stick is a stick until it can actually be used for something fun, like softball. Hunt around for a stick or branch that would work as a softball bat. Anything that's two to three feet in length and one to three inches in diameter is great. Bonus points if you can find one with a broader top and a narrower handle. Then get some batting practice in by smacking some tennis or whiffle balls around.

3. TARGET PRACTICE

Stumps or large logs are just what you need for target practice. Find a handful of small- and medium-size stones, and then throw them at the stump or log. How many of your throws hit the wood? If most or all of them hit, try moving back and seeing if you can still be accurate. If you want to build your sharpshooting skills even more, draw a target with different point values on the wood with chalk. How many points can you rack up with ten shots?

4. CLAIM A WALKING STICK

A gnarly, big walking stick that's all your own makes any hike way more fun. Go on a hunt for the perfect walking stick candidate–you want one that's about as tall as your arm when it's extended and sturdy enough to lean on without it snapping. Once you have a good contender, groom it for greatness by snapping off any small branches, scraping off any moss, or writing your name on it in chalk or wrapping it with colorful tape. You can also ask an adult to help you carve off the bark with a knife if you want a smooth, bark-free stick.

5. PRACTICE WHITTLING

If you find a small piece of wood that fits in your hand, it might be the perfect piece to practice whittling on. You definitely want an adult around if you're handling a pocketknife, and make sure you hold only the back of the wood and move your knife away from you, never toward you, so you don't end up whittling your hand. If it's your first time, try carving a pencil by sharpening one of the long edges. As you get more advanced, you can practice carving simple shapes like an egg or a snowman out of bigger chunks of wood.

HOW TO BUILD A FORT, INDOORS AND OUT

People have been building forts and strongholds since ancient times for protection, trade, festivals, and more. These impressive buildings come in all shapes and sizes. Some are short and squat, like Florida's turtle-shaped fort called the Castillo de San Marcos. Others are tall and grand, like the Spanish castle Alcazar de Segovia, which looks like a castle out of a fairy tale.

Anywhere you go in the world, people have built forts, and that's because there's nothing better than having your own hideaway from the world. A place where you can tuck yourself in with all your coziest blankets and pillows, surround yourself with your favorite books, games, and toys, stock up on the yummiest snacks, and just hang out and relax for a few hours.

A fort—either indoors or out—is the perfect place to get away to when you want to be by yourself, and it's also the perfect place to camp out with a brother or sister or friends and play games or listen to music together. And the very best thing about a fort? It can be built anyplace you want, with anything you want—the sky's the limit for your architectural vision!

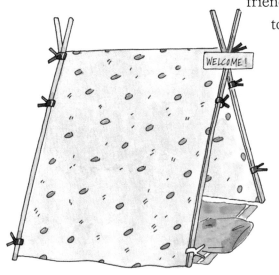

WELCOME!

HOW TO BUILD A COZY LIVING ROOM HIDEAWAY

BASIC MATERIALS

- **3 pieces of furniture**
- **2 to 4 sheets or blankets**
- **Pillows**
- **3 heavy objects, such as books**
- **1 to 2 comforters or sleeping bags**

EXTRA MATERIALS

- **String lights or flashlight**
- **Clothespins**
- **More pillows and blankets**
- **Broom or something else that is long and tall**
- **Snacks, books, and games**

INSTRUCTIONS

1. Arrange your furniture into a triangular shape. Try using a couch and then adding two chairs.

2. Toss your sheets and blankets over the furniture one at a time. Keep adding blankets until the top and sides are covered.

3. To keep the roof taut, use some heavy objects to weigh down each corner. Now your basic structure is ready and it's time to decorate!

4. Put all of your other blankets, pillows, and sleeping bags inside your fort. Spread out the blankets, plump up your pillows, and lay out your sleeping bags until you like how everything's laid out.

5. Then bring in reinforcements! Is it a little too dark? Add some fairy lights. Want the roof to be higher? Use a broom leaned on a chair to prop up the center of the fort. Need to stock your fort's "refrigerator"? Fill a box or bin with your favorite snacks and sips and set it up in a "kitchen" corner of your space. The beauty of a fort is that it's *your* secret hideaway from the world, so make it as cozy, comfy, or kooky as you want!

HOW TO BUILD AN UNDER-THE-STARS FORTRESS

BASIC MATERIALS

- **Clothesline or rope**
- **Sheets and blankets**
- **Binder clips, rubber bands, or twine**
- **Pillows and extra blankets**

EXTRA MATERIALS

- **Flashlights or lanterns**
- **Snacks, books, and games**
- **Weights, such as heavy books**
- **Large cardboard boxes**

INSTRUCTIONS

1. Spend some time scouting for the ideal location. Be on the lookout for areas with trees or other structures that you can hang things from or lean things against.

2. Once you find your location, start setting up the structure for your fortress. You can custom craft your fort to fit your location, your building materials, and your architectural vision—this is your fort, so anything goes! Or, if you want to keep things simple, you can go for a classic A-frame tent fort. Just stretch a piece of rope from one tree branch or trunk to another, about 3 to 4 feet off the ground. This is the main beam of your A-frame fort, and when you fold a big blanket over it, you'll have a classic tent fort.

3. Whatever you're using for the bones of your fort, start laying your sheets and blankets on this supporting structure to create a roof and sides. You can use supplies like twine or rubber bands to fasten the blankets better, or add them to your base structure if it seems wobbly. You can also use weights, like heavy books, to pin blanket corners down to the ground.

4. Adjust the fort until it seems stable, then your basic fort is done. Now it's decorating time! You can transform your fortress into anything you can imagine, like a personal library, a theater, a studio, a nap spot, or anything else you want it to be. You can also add on more wings to your main fort by adding a few cardboard box additions. Maybe you can store books in one wing for your library, snacks in another for your kitchen, and extra pillows in another for your nap room. How many different kinds of hideouts can you design?

HOW TO HAMMER A NAIL

Hammering a nail is one of the first skills you'll want to learn as a builder, since it'll form the foundation of the many bookshelves, tables, benches, and other fun things you'll be able to build soon. When you're getting started, make sure you have an adult nearby, just in case that hammer lands on a finger and not a nail!

Start by holding the hammer near the end of the handle. Try not to hold it close to the head. The closer to the end of the handle you hold, the harder you can strike, just as the longer the handle, the harder the blow. Use light strokes—just taps—to start the nail. After you're sure the nail is going in straight, you can then use more force to drive it in. But don't try to sink the nailhead completely flush with the wood—it's OK if it sticks up a little bit. That's because if you keep hammering, you'll start hitting the wood, and any dent or depression in the wood will probably show in the finished piece.

When you're swinging your hammer, try to swing the head back and forth in an arc, with your wrist steady at the center. Focus on trying to keep your arc steady and fluid with each hit. It may seem to take a long time, but before you know it, your nail will be hammered in much more quickly and straighter than if you took short taps or swung all over the place.

Another thing to work on is trying to keep your wrist steady and the hammerhead parallel with the top of the nail when you're hitting the nail. Try starting your swing with the hammerhead down squarely on the nail and the handle parallel to the top of the nail. Then pull back and swing through your practiced arc. This will help you keep your nail straight. If your wrist and hammer aren't parallel with the nailhead at the start, you're more likely to hit the nail crookedly or bend it when you swing back down.

It's a great idea to do a little hammering practice on a piece of scrap wood so you can work on your aim. It's not as easy as it seems to hit the same spot over and over when you're swinging a heavy hammer, so don't get frustrated if your hammering is a little all over the place at first. Try practicing your arc motion on a soft piece of wood to see how close you can get to hitting the same spot with every swing.

Sometimes a nail just doesn't want to go in straight, and it can get bent and go in the wrong direction. If you pull it out, don't try to hammer another nail in the same hole—instead, start over in another spot. Nails bend for a lot of reasons that are usually easy to fix. A nail can bend if the face of the hammerhead has glue or grease on it. If you have a few nails in a row that are going in crooked, make sure you check if there's anything on your hammerhead that's making it slip. If that happens, rub it on a piece of fine sandpaper or wash with soap, water, and a scrub brush.

Sometimes a nail is getting bent because the hammer is just too heavy for you—that's actually one of the most common reasons why your aim can get wobbly! If so, go for a hammer that's a comfier size for you and that feels heavy, but not too heavy, in your hand, and that you can swing in an arc without hurting your wrist. A clean, nice-size hammer is the secret ingredient to dozens of super-fun woodworking projects!

GRAB A GROWN-UP!

BUILD YOUR OWN RACE CAR

How fast do you think the fastest race car on earth can go? The answer is . . . over 230 miles per hour! That's more than three times faster than a cheetah, the world's fastest land animal, which can run up to seventy miles per hour. And it's also three times faster than we drive when we're on the highway. It's mind-boggling to see how fast race cars can go, which is why hundreds of thousands of people flock to stock car races to watch the drivers zoom by and jockey for first place. It takes years of training to master race car driving, but if you have the need for speed, you can also get your thrills by building your own toy car and hosting a grand prix at home. (Don't forget to ask an adult to help with the drilling part of your car construction!) Who knows, you could be the next Danica Patrick, the first woman in history to win a prestigious IndyCar race.

MATERIALS

- **Milk or juice carton**
- **Scissors**
- **2 (3-millimeter diameter) skewers**
- **Marker**
- **4 plastic bottle caps**
- **Drill and 7/64-inch drill bit**
- **Hot glue gun**
- **Decorations, such as paint, washi tape, or glitter (optional)**
- **1 straw**
- **Balloon**
- **Masking tape**

INSTRUCTIONS

1. Cut the milk or juice carton in half lengthwise. This will be the body of your car.

2. Lay the box down with the wide side facing up. Place your skewers on the box so that they stretch across the shortest distance and are parallel to each other. These will be your car's axles.

3. With the marker, make dots on the box underneath of the end of each skewer. Mark the four dots close to the edge of the box so that your wheels (the bottle caps) will be able to touch the ground.

4. Poke holes at each dot and then push your skewers through the holes.

5. Cut the ends of the skewers so that 1½ to 2 inches of the axle sticks out from each hole.

6. Take the bottle caps and have an adult help you drill a hole through the center of the bottle caps with a 7/64-inch drill bit.

7. Push a bottle cap onto each skewer and dab a little hot glue where the skewer pokes through the bottle cap. This will secure your wheels to your axles.

8. Time to decorate! If you want to jazz up your car, try painting the body with racing stripes, wrapping it in washi tape, adding glitter, or decorating it however speaks to you.

9. Grab a straw and cut it so it's about 1 inch longer than the car's body. If your box is longer than the straw, you can leave the straw as it is.

10. Place one end of the straw into the balloon and tape the balloon closed around the straw. Now you have an engine!

11. Tape the straw on top of the car so the balloon is at the front of the car and the open end of the straw is at the back. Make sure the straw sticks out over the front of the car a little so that you can blow air into it.

12. To fill the balloon, hold the straw to your mouth and place your other hand where the balloon is taped to the straw. Blow into the straw until the balloon is full of air, then pinch the balloon's opening to keep the air in until you're ready to race.

13. Your miniature racer is ready to hit the track. To start your car, release your finger from the balloon so the air trapped inside the balloon propels your car forward. Grab a stopwatch and see how long it takes your car to zip from one end of your designated track to another. How fast can you get it to go? Record your best time, then make some tweaks to your design, like adding a cardboard fin or an extra set of wheels. What makes your car go fastest?

BUILD A BENCH IN AN AFTERNOON

The first bench ever invented was . . . probably just a log. Technically, a bench is any seating for two or more people, so almost anything—from a stoop to a windowsill—can be a bench. In the past, when all furniture was handmade and expensive, benches were the seats of the masses and chairs were reserved for only the most important people. (That's where we get the word "chairwoman" from!)

But today, most furniture is designed by people, built by machines, and mass-produced to make sure we can all have comfortable seating at affordable prices. Logging and milling have also radically improved, meaning that anyone can buy sturdy, smooth, build-worthy wood at the hardware store for just a few dollars. That means anyone can become a furniture designer and builder these days, and with the right tools and plans (and some adult help), you can launch your woodworking career in just a weekend.

MATERIALS

- 1 (2 by 8 by 96-inch) board
- 2 (2 by 4 by 96-inch) boards
- Tape measure
- Pencil
- Handsaw or miter saw
- Drill
- 32 (2½-inch) screws
- Sanding block
- Wood stain and brush (optional)

INSTRUCTIONS

1. Take the 2 by 4-inch boards and measure out four 10-inch-long sections and four 16-inch-long sections. Make sure to mark each section with a pencil, and remember, always measure twice so you only have to cut once!

2. Using a handsaw and with help from an adult, cut the boards at your section markers and put

them to the side. If using a miter saw, ask an adult to handle the cuts for you.

3. Grab two 10-inch boards and one 16-inch board. On the floor, place the 10-inch boards upright, 16 inches apart, and parallel to each other so the 4-inch sides of the board face one another. Then place the 16-inch board at the top to form three sides of a rectangle with flush sides.

4. With help from your adult, and holding the 10-inch boards in place, drill pilot holes at the four corners of the top of the 16-inch board. A pilot hole is a small hole you drill into wood before drilling in a screw. This helps displace the wood so there's room for the screw to drive in.

5. Again, holding the 10-inch boards in place, drill screws into the pilot holes, one side at a time. Now your three boards should be secured together with screws.

6. Flip the structure over and attach another 16-inch board to the other side using the same process. You should now have a closed rectangle that is 16 inches long and 14 inches wide. Your bench's first leg is done!

7. Repeat steps 3 through 6 to make a second leg. Set the legs aside.

8. Take your two 2 by 8 by 48-inch boards and lay them side by side. They should lay flush against each other and form a rectangle that's 4 feet tall and 16 inches wide. This is the bench seat.

9. Place the bench legs on top of the seat so the short side of the leg is touching the bench seat. The open part of the legs will face each other.

10. Measure and move the legs as needed so that each leg is 4 inches from the end of the seat. The legs should also be centered in the other direction, so that there is 1 inch of space between the long edge of the seat and the leg.

11. Once in place, drill eight evenly spaced pilot holes through the leg and into the seat.

12. Drill screws through the leg and into the seat. The leg is now attached to the seat!

13. Repeat steps 11 and 12 for the second bench leg.

14. Flip the bench over and sand it thoroughly using the sanding block.

15. If you want to take your design further, stain it with a wood stain or paint it in your favorite color of latex paint and then seal it so it's safe to sit on. Your bench is now complete!

CHAPTER 6:

Let's Be Chefs!

Chefs are on an endless quest for one thing: flavor. Like scientists, chefs are constantly experimenting with new techniques, ingredients, and recipes, all in service to cooking and eating delicious food. Chefs are hands-on with food every single day, but they also use their senses of taste, smell, sight, and sound to tell when something is perfectly cooked and ready to eat. The best way to become a master chef is to just jump into the kitchen and cook a few recipes. The more you cook and the more you eat, the more you'll see how food is also an art form and a powerful way to express yourself.

THE HANDS-ON GIRL'S KITCHEN

If you've ever walked through the cookbook section at a bookstore, then you can see how there must be hundreds of thousands of recipes in the world. But even though there are an endless number of ways to put food together, most of the time, you don't need anything too fancy to create something delicious. You probably already own everything you need to make 90 percent of the recipes out there, but as you keep exploring and building your culinary instincts, you might want to test out other interesting tools like those in the upgraded kitchen list below.

THE STARTUP KITCHEN

You don't need a lot to start cooking, but there are a few essential items that you can't get by without. These tools are most likely already in your kitchen or can be found at your local grocery store.

- [ ] **Mixing bowls**
- [ ] **Mixing spoons**
- [ ] **Measuring cups**
- [ ] **Measuring spoons**
- [ ] **Knife (see page 179 to find a knife that's right for you)**
- [ ] **Vegetable peeler**
- [ ] **Cutting board**
- [ ] **Large pot**
- [ ] **Large pan**
- [ ] **Colander**

- [ ] **Baking sheet**
- [ ] **Whisk**
- [ ] **Oven and stovetop**

THE UPGRADED KITCHEN

Cooking was done completely by hand for centuries, but people are always inventing gadgets to make things a little easier. Here are some of those useful inventions, but remember—they're totally optional!

- [ ] **Food processor**
- [ ] **Food scale**
- [ ] **Hand mixer or stand mixer**
- [ ] **Blender**
- [ ] **Cookie cutters**
- [ ] **Cheese grater**
- [ ] **Silicone spatula**
- [ ] **Ice cream scoop**
- [ ] **Basting brush**
- [ ] **Garlic press**
- [ ] **Bench scraper**
- [ ] **Glass storage jars**
- [ ] **Apron**

VEGETABLE GARDENING 101

If you've ever plucked a sun-warmed cherry tomato straight off the plant and popped it in your mouth, you know how wonderfully delicious garden-fresh veggies are. That's because almost all of the vegetables at the grocery store spend weeks in warehouses, trucks, and at the store before they make it to your table. So sometimes their flavor has dulled.

But having that same vegetable fresh from the garden is like eating an entirely different thing. And the best part is that it's super fun to plant your own garden and tend to it with your new gardening skills. Just follow the tips below once spring rolls around, and, in just a few weeks, you'll be snacking on all your favorite veggies, grown by you!

TIMING

We all know spring is the best time to kick off a garden, but how do we know if our veggies will be happy in March, April, May, or not until June or later? That's a question gardeners have asked themselves for centuries, which is why the handy Hardiness Zone system was invented. This system has organized the entire United States into thirteen zones, depending on the average minimum temperature. Zone 1 (-60 to -50°F) would be the northern part of Alaska; Zone 13 (60 to 70°F) would be the southern part of Puerto Rico; Zone 7 would be temperate areas like North Carolina.

You can find out your zone by searching online for the "Garden. org USDA Hardiness Zone Finder." There you can type in your zip code, find out what zone or subzone you're in, and even find a customized planting calendar, telling you exactly when to plant each vegetable in your area. You'll see from the planting calendar that it's actually best to stagger your plantings–things like lettuce can go in early and handle colder temperatures—so that your garden is planted in a few smaller batches instead of all in one day.

LOCATION

The next question gardeners ask themselves is: where should all my plants go? If you're sticking to indoor or deck gardening, the easy answer might be in a container in the sunniest spot where you can fit it. If you want to plant perennials, which are plants that grow back on their own every year (like asparagus or rhubarb), then you might also want to keep them in their own containers or another permanent spot. That way, they'll have their own safe little home to bloom every year.

But if you have space to plant a bigger garden of annuals, which don't regrow each year, you'll have to answer a few more questions. First, where do you have an open space, away from too many trees or shrubs that will cast shade? Second, which way is the light coming from? A garden that faces south always gets the best light, so maybe that means planting your patch horizontally, vertically, or at an angle so you can capture that sweet southern sun. Usually you want a spot that gets six to eight hours of sun each day, but if you get a little less, there are still veggies, like lettuce and spinach, that will do just fine there.

Whatever way you place your garden to get the best sun, make sure to plant tall veggies, like tomatoes, pole beans, and anything else that needs a trellis, at the back (north side) of your garden, so they don't shade the little guys in the front.

SIZE

Once you have a spot in mind, you'll have to figure out how big you want your new garden to be. It's really tempting to plant a big garden and have tons of veggies, but you have to consider how much upkeep you're willing to do (think about all the weeding!). It's better to start by asking yourself how many tomatoes, heads of lettuce, broccoli, or whatever else you think you and your family can realistically eat this summer. It's always better to start small so it doesn't get overwhelming—after all, you can plant more next summer once you've got a green thumb. Whatever size you choose, make sure none of your rows or your bed are wider than four feet, or it'll be hard to reach weeds deep inside your garden.

SOIL

If we want our food to be delicious, we have to give it food of its own. And what plants like is nutrient-rich soil! Luckily, it's easy to buy a nutrient-packed soil buffet for plants at most hardware stores in big bags, and the blends are customized, so you don't have to sit there and meal plan for your plants. All you have to do is calculate how much soil you need by multiplying the length, width, and depth of your garden patch or bed. So a 4-foot by 8-foot, 2-foot-deep bed would need 64 cubic feet of soil.

If you're lucky enough to live in a place with naturally rich, dark soil, then skip the store-bought stuff and just till up what you have. Make sure you also spot and toss out any rocks or stones that could block your plant roots from growing. You might also want to mix in some compost or fertilizer to make your plants extra happy.

SEEDS OR TRANSPLANTS?

We can't have veggies without seeds, right? Well, actually, you can! You can skip the seeding step if you buy transplants, which are just partially grown plants that someone has started for you already. You can find most popular veggies, like tomatoes, lettuce, and herbs, as partially grown plants, and if it's your first time gardening, this is a great way to make it easier and up your chances of a great harvest. That's because transplants have already gotten past their baby stage, when they're more at risk of dying, so they're like sturdy, tough little warriors who are ready to make it out in the real world of your garden.

The downside to starting from transplants is that you won't have as much variety, since most garden stores keep only a handful of varieties of each vegetable and usually won't have transplants of things like broccoli or cauliflower. But when you enter the wide world of seeds, you'll have literally thousands of vegetables and varieties to choose from—any plant you like to eat, you can buy its seeds. And with just a little bit of patience, you can grow your own mini transplants that will be ready to pop into the garden once the weather warms up.

If you want to take on growing veggies from seed instead of buying transplants, start early in the spring or late in the winter, depending on your zone, by planting your seeds in a seedling tray (or recycled small pots like yogurt containers with drainage holes poked in the bottom!) filled with seed-starting mix. Plant a few seeds per pot to up your chances of success and follow the directions on the packet to know how deep to plant each type of seed. Set your little veggie nursery in a sunny, warm spot until you see a few leaves sprout, then move it to a cooler but still sunny location to help the plant get hardy. Once you have two sets of leaves on each plant, you can thin out any extra plants that have sprouted and keep just one strong plant per pot. And as soon as your planting calendar says it's safe to transplant your seedlings, go ahead and unleash them on the world of your garden!

THE EIGHT EASIEST VEGETABLES TO GROW

Planting a garden, and especially a vegetable garden, can seem pretty intimidating at first. It seems like there are so many things each plant needs, from certain temperatures, to the right amount of water, to a mix of nutrients in the soil, to weeding and pest control.

But the truth is vegetable gardening can actually be super simple. Vegetables really need just three things: sun, water, and soil. And most are pretty forgiving about the quantities of each of those things too. As long as you choose a sunny spot, do some daily watering, and use a store-bought soil mix, you'll have a great chance of growing beautiful, delicious, showstopping vegetables.

Most hardware stores will have an awesome display of young plants in early spring and lots of varieties of seeds all year round, and half the fun is reading all the tags and dreaming up what you want to eat this year. Maybe this will be the year you grow your own gourmet salads with lettuce, tomatoes, and cucumbers. Maybe you'll specialize in herbs (if so, see page 169 for a handy herb guide!). But what should you plant when there are so many options? Well, if you can dream it, and if you like to eat it, you can grow it. And if you want easy, impressive, yummy vegetables all summer long, start out with these eight favorite, effortless veggies.

1. LETTUCE

Did you know you can grow your own salad without much work at all? Lettuce is one of the easiest vegetables to grow and also one of the easiest to use in everything from chopped salad to salad wraps to lettuce soup (yes, it's a thing!). Lettuce is also amazing because there are so many types of it—from the iceberg and romaine we see all the time to fancy, frilly kinds like Ruby Gem and Flashy Butter Oak. Lettuce loves colder temperatures, so you can start it in early spring. But you can also find types of lettuce that don't mind some heat and can grow all summer long. Look for a plant with springy, brightly colored leaves, plant it according to the instructions on the tag, and in three to four weeks, you'll be harvesting your own farm-fresh salads.

2. TOMATOES

Tomatoes are one of the most popular starter vegetables for a garden because they're so easy to grow, they're especially delicious when homegrown, and they can take up as much or as little space as you have available. If you're starting out with a container garden, try cherry or grape tomatoes, like Sungolds or Golden Sweets (don't forget to use tomato cages in your containers—these plants can grow up to six feet tall!). If you have a patch of garden or raised beds, try large, meaty tomatoes like Early Girls and Big Boys, which love crawling their vines up stakes. There are also hundreds of heirloom tomato varieties that are native to different parts of the country—try searching for "heirloom seeds" along with your county or state to see what unique variety might have been born right in your home state.

3. SPINACH AND KALE

Spinach, kale, and their other leafy cousins are other fun vegetables to grow because they can be used in so many ways in the kitchen. You can sauté them into creamy, cheesy veggie dip; you can whir them in a smoothie; you can add them to basil for a fresh, springy pesto. And even better, you can also replace them with their cousins in most recipes. Maybe you want to experiment with the pepperiness of arugula or watercress, or the pretty pop of purple of radicchio or endive. Or do you want to try adventurous varieties like mizuna, tatsoi, or mâche? Whatever leafy greens you choose, remember that they can differ in what time of year you should plant them—spinach and kale, for instance, love the cold—so read your plant tags and seed envelopes before you select a species.

4. PEPPERS

Peppers are another place you can go wild in your garden. Try red and yellow bell peppers, which are sweet and snappy. Or pop a few mini snacking peppers in your garden, which make a perfect dipper for hummus, ranch, or salsa and also look super cute in fajitas and tacos. Or maybe you're ready to handle some heat. Plant jalapeños, which grow great in pots but need plenty of water (you will too when you take that first five-alarm bite!). Many hot peppers, like jalapeños, love the heat themselves, so they'll do best in temperatures between 65ºF and 90ºF. But nothing spices up dinner like knowing you've grown a little part of taco night yourself.

5. ZUCCHINI

Zucchini, and its cousin, squash, are the butt of a popular gardening joke: which is that you can't give the stuff away in the summer. That's because zucchini grows quickly, easily, and everywhere, and if you blink, it might just take over your garden and your fridge. But that's also what makes it such a fun vegetable to grow—you can get dozens of zucchinis off of one plant all summer long, and there are a thousand ways to use it. Try spiralizing it into zoodles, or slicing it thin, coating it in parmesan, and baking it for cheesy crisps, or grating it into your favorite chocolate chip muffin recipe. Just remember: one plant should give you plenty, and you want to harvest them when they're still small and flavorful, before they turn into the dreaded flavorless monster zuke!

6. CUCUMBERS

You might think cucumbers like to stay cool as, well, a cucumber, but these members of the gourd family are actually all about that warm weather. But not too hot—temperatures that stay in the 90s can stress them out and give you fewer cukes to harvest. Even though they're a little finicky about temperature, everything else about cukes is a snap. They love plenty of water, sunlight, and trellis support, so they'll cozy right up to any tomatoes you have. And of course, being able to turn them into homemade pickles on burgers, cool and tangy tzatziki, and freshly sliced rounds for dipping make them the coolest, crunchiest things in your kitchen.

7. CARROTS

Another favorite little dipper, carrots grow underground, like potatoes and onions. This makes them a fun experiment in sowing and harvesting—you can plant them, wait seventy to eighty days, pull up your beautiful, fresh carrots, then start all over again. Try changing a few variables each time you plant. How do they grow when you plant them closer together? How do they grow early in the spring versus in the heat of summer? You can plant yellow, white, purple, and even crimson carrots, and they're all equally delicious for dipping in ranch, shredding into salads and slaw, or roasting with a favorite spice mix. But the one variety you can't plant? Baby carrots. That's because baby carrots are actually just big carrots that have been whittled down into bite-size shapes.

8. MARIGOLDS

Why would a flower be on a list of easy vegetables to grow? Because it's one of the plants that will make it easier to grow those vegetables. Marigolds are miracle workers at keeping pesky pests away from your garden—their unique chemical composition keeps many bad bugs away, both above and below the ground, all without pesticides. They even keep the cute but destructive pests, like rabbits, away from your garden so you don't end up growing a salad bar for the bunnies with nothing for yourself. Plant several in the corners of your garden then step back and admire your work—aren't they pretty? And every time you remember that they're doing the dirty work of pest control for you, you'll love them even more.

HERBS AND HOW TO CARE FOR THEM

Herbs are the perfect project if you're just starting out gardening because, for one, they're small! They fit just right in a small pot on a windowsill, and they're also super easy to take care of and much less fussy than vegetables. And the best part? You can enjoy their tasty leaves straight off the stem. Herbs add a ton of flavor to food, and there's nothing like popping a mint leaf into your glass of water or sprinkling a little bit of fresh parsley on your scrambled eggs. Nearly every food has some kind of herb, fresh or dried, added to it. Pizza sauce has plenty of basil; tacos get their taco-y flavor in part from dried oregano, and mint chocolate chip ice cream? Mint leaves, of course! So, are you ready to embark on an herbaceous adventure? Pick a favorite herb from the list below, and let's start potting, watering, and munching.

BASIL

Basil—that yummy herb in most of our favorite pizza and pasta sauces—is one the easiest herbs to grow. It loves plenty of water (but not on its leaves), so you'll want to water it at the base every one to two days to keep the soil moist. To check the moisture, stick your finger in the soil up to your first knuckle. If it's dry, it's time for some watering can rain. Because basil also likes warm temperatures (over 50ºF) and lots of sunlight, place your pot near a window that's facing south or west so it can enjoy all those rays.

PARSLEY

Chefs love to garnish their dishes with a sprinkle of parsley because it's delicious and adds a pretty pop of green to any plate. Parsley is the go-to herb for a chef-y gardener, and it's also easy to grow. It likes plenty of sun, like basil, but can handle much colder temperatures (it can even survive snow!). Parsley needs a medium amount of water—as long as the soil is moist but not soggy, it'll be happy. You can choose from two kinds of parsley to grow: Italian (also called flat parsley) and curly parsley. Both taste great, so choose whichever one looks most interesting to you.

MINT

Mint is an herb that you always want to grow in its own container. It can't resist spreading and taking over everything. In fact, if you plant it in a garden bed or other open space, you'll end up with a forest of mint. Mint is happiest in full sun, but it can handle partial sun too, so you can even place it in an east- or north-facing window. Although mint prefers moist soil, it's much hardier than most herbs when it comes to water and won't quit on you if it gets a little dried out every now and then.

OREGANO

Another favorite herb for Italian and Mexican cooking, oregano has a rich and savory flavor. This laid-back herb only needs a pot that's twelve inches wide and some sunshine to grow like crazy. Its flavor is strongest if it can get a full day of sunshine, but it'll be perfectly happy and yummy with partial sun. This herb needs little water and only wants a drink when the soil feels dry to the touch. That means that once you have your right-size pot and your sunny spot, you can be mostly hands-off, except for occasional watering. (Good luck staying hands-off the harvest, though—fresh oregano is awesome on both take-out and homemade pizza slices!)

CILANTRO

Cilantro is both the superhero and supervillain of the herb world. This divisive herb has a chemical compound that can taste like soap to a small percentage of people with certain genes. Even within a family, some people can have the soapy cilantro gene while others don't! But for those who don't, cilantro is the delicious flavor backbone of foods like salsa verde, chimichurri, and Vietnamese bún. Cilantro dislikes direct sunlight—no southern windows for this guy—so keep it at a window that's bright but not sun-seared. It likes a moist soil but needs plenty of drainage because of its big root system. Make sure to use a pot that drains well (or place a layer of pebbles at the bottom of the pot to help with drainage). And did you know? Cilantro and coriander are actually the same plant! So if you see either one at the garden store, snatch it up.

THE PERFECT PROVISIONS FOR ADVENTURES

When you're planning your next hike or camping trip, it's fun to daydream about all the things you're going to see and all the delicious camping grub you're going to chow down on! There's nothing like having a backpack filled with snacks when you're on the trail, or a cooler stocked with your favorite provisions to pillage once you're back at camp. After all, food and adventure go hand in hand, since you need all the energy you can get when you're you on the trail.

Campsite cooking is all about keeping it simple and eating your favorite, filling, energy-packed meals without any fuss. To minimize the chaos, try out this cheat sheet next time you help plan and pack up for an adventure.

WHAT TO BRING FOR A HIKE

Whether it's a thirty-minute nature walk or a three-hour mountain hike, you don't want to leave home without these snacking basics.

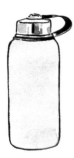

WATER

This is the most important one! Never set off an adventure without a bottle of water, because you can't have any fun if you're parched. Carry the biggest bottle you can handle without it weighing you down or look for one that you can slide into a backpack pocket for easier hauling.

TRAIL MIX

Trail mix is a trail classic because it works.
It packs you full of energy to pound out
miles of hiking. But it's especially delicious
when you customize it with the ingredients
you most love. Look for ideas for making
your own signature trail mix on page 185.

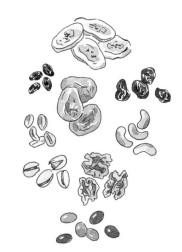

JERKY

Jerky is a protein-packed treat that keeps you feeling full and
high-energy for hours. Because jerky is dehydrated, it can last a
long time without going bad in most temperatures. Store-bought
jerky comes in dozens of flavors, but it's also surprisingly easy to
make your own—see page 184 for our favorite jerky recipe.

FRUIT AND PEANUT BUTTER

Who doesn't love apples or bananas with peanut butter? Lucky
for us, they also make a great extra-energy snack for the trail.
The protein in peanut butter will keep you from getting hungry
too quickly, and we all know fruits are packed with nutritious
vitamins. Plus, is there anything easier than grabbing a banana or
apple from the fruit bowl on your way out the door?

OVERNIGHT

If you're off on a longer adventure, like an overnight or weekend
camping trip, you'll have to pack more provisions. And the best
way to make sure you'll have something *you* want to eat at camp?
Pitch in with the planning and packing! Here are a few campsite
staples that are super easy to make but still delicious, fun, and
something to look forward to after a long day of exploration.

DINNER

CLASSIC: HOT DOGS AND BURGERS

What's better than roasting a weenie over a campfire? Keep it simple by packing a few packages of beef, turkey, or veggie hot dogs, hot dog buns, and ketchup and mustard. Or get fancy with loaded hot dogs, topped with chili, cheese sauce, coleslaw, onions, relish, and anything else you like on your dog. If you want more variety, you can also throw a few burger patties, buns, and slices of cheese into the cooler for a burger–dog night. Just don't forget that anytime you're doing live-fire cooking, you'll want an adult nearby to be your sous chef.

TWIST: SAUCY SALSA CHICKEN BURRITOS

Chicken burritos are nearly as easy to make as burgers because, just like burgers, they're a grilled meat wrapped up in some carb-y goodness. But they can be a fun change of pace from the old standby, and you can make them as simple or as fancy as you want. Before cooking the chicken on the grill with your grown-up's help, keep it simple by seasoning it with some oil, salt, and pepper, or marinate it in salsa in a plastic baggie at home so it arrives at camp with extra-ramped-up flavor. At home, chop any toppings you want, like lettuce, tomatoes, or black olives, then toss the containers of tortillas, cheese, sour cream, and salsa straight from your grocery bag into your cooler. Wrangling a burrito by the campfire also makes for a fun challenge; and, hey, if the tortilla breaks and salsa goes everywhere, who cares? You're outside!

BREAKFAST
CLASSIC: SCRAMBLED EGGS AND BACON

All you need for this campsite classic is a carton of eggs, plenty of bacon, and a heavy fireproof skillet. Cook your bacon first until its browned and crispy, then ask for help to pour off most of the fat into a container, leaving some of it to cook your eggs. Scramble your eggs right in the bacon fat and crispy leftover bits, add salt and pepper, and pile it all high on your plate. Now that's a hearty breakfast to kick off the day.

TWIST: BUILD YOUR OWN FLAPJACK BAR

Weekend mornings are made for pancakes, and camping doesn't change that. Just like at home, campsite flapjacks are fluffy, sweet, and oh-so-toppable. You can pack store-bought pancake mix (that'll save cooler space!) or make your own by mixing flour, sugar, baking soda, baking powder, and salt. You can also premix milk and eggs in a jar or bottle, keep it in the cooler, and stir it into your dry ingredients once it's fireside pancake time. Don't forget to bring a mixing bowl and a stash of butter, syrup, and other fun toppings like berries, bananas, whipped cream, chocolate chips, honey, or whatever else you like. Finally, set all your toppings out in an assembly line so each person can build the flapjack of their dreams.

THREE KINDS OF COOKING
AND WHEN TO USE THEM

Are there some cooking nights you love? Maybe you have a regular pizza night or Taco Tuesday or one thing your grown-up makes that's just *the best.* Whether it's baking a homemade pizza or loading up your tacos with your favorite fillings, there are actually all different kinds of cooking that go into your weekly dinners. And each type of cooking has its own special use—that's why we wouldn't boil a burrito or grill a pie! Here are the five kinds of cooking and when to employ them.

1. ROASTING AND BAKING

Roasting and baking are two sides of the same coin—they both happen in the oven, usually at a temperature between 250 and 450°F. But we usually say roasting when we're talking about savory food like chicken and casseroles, while baking refers to breads, pizza, and desserts. They're also both forms of dry-heat cooking.

Dry-heat cooking is when you don't add any liquid, like water or broth, while you're cooking. That's why it's perfect if you want to crisp something up or dry a wet batter so it becomes a solid cake. The dryness in the air of the oven sucks moisture away from your food—like the natural water content in a carrot or chicken, or the milk you added to your cake batter—and either browns and crisps the food (so you get crispy carrots and browned chicken) or lets the other ingredients soak up that liquid (so you get a moist cake instead of a runny batter). It's perfect if you want a more hands-off method of cooking, where you don't need to stand over the stove. But it can also take more time than some of the other methods, and it usually doesn't brown food as much as sautéing can.

2. SAUTÉING AND FRYING

Sautéing is a fancy French word for frying something in a pan with a little bit of fat. It means "jump" in French, and that's because when you're sautéing at the stovetop, you're usually moving the food around in the pan much more than if you were cooking it in the oven. The point of sautéing is to brown your food (have you noticed how the brown, crispy parts of food taste so good?), which caramelizes the natural sugars that exist in every ingredient and makes their flavor deeper and yummier. You can also brown food on the grill (that's why the grill marks on chicken are darker—the parts of the meat that touched the grates have caramelized).

Frying is a lot like sautéing, except you're adding a lot more fat, such as oil or butter. A shallow or pan fry is when the food is partially covered with fat, and a deep fry is when the food is completely covered or dipped right into the cooking fat. Anywhere the food comes in contact with heat and fat, it will get browner and crispier, which is why deep-fried chicken tenders are brown and crispy all over, but pan-fried chicken breast might be brown and crispy only where it touched the pan.

3. BOILING AND STEAMING

We've all seen eggs being boiled, right? But have you thought about how and why they go from runny and goopy to firm and bitable? It's because the water in the pot, which boils at 212°F, is surrounding the egg and heating it up from the outside until it cooks and hardens. That's what boiling, and its cousins, poaching, steaming, and simmering, are all about—using the power of hot water to cook things while adding plenty of moisture. This is also called moist-heat cooking.

If that same egg isn't protected by its shell, you would be poaching it, not boiling it. Poaching is cooking in water at a lower temperature than boiling—between 140 and 180°F—which produces fewer bubbles that won't rip the egg to shreds before it cooks. If you have something a little sturdier than an egg, like rice or beans, you might simmer them, which is cooking in liquid at just below boiling temperature, which produces tiny bubbles.

If you have a delicate piece of fish, like halibut, you might go for steaming instead. With steaming, the food avoids direct contact with water and instead cooks from the heat given off by the steam, usually while water boils right below it. Any kind of wet heat cooking is perfect if you want the flavor of an ingredient to shine through—it won't produce any kind of browning, so all you taste is the bright, direct flavor of that food.

RAINY DAY ACTIVITY

THE ONE-HOUR DIY KNIFE SKILLS CLASS

All of those chefs you see on TV chopping, slicing, and dicing at lightning fast speed have one thing in common: they've put hours of training into honing their knife skills. One of the first things aspiring chefs are taught at culinary school is how to wield a knife safely and chop quickly. But in just one hour, with a few tools and an adult to help, you can enroll in your own culinary-school-inspired Knife Skills 101 class at home. So welcome to class—here's what you'll need!

HOW DO YOU KNOW WHICH KNIFE IS RIGHT FOR YOU?

Chefs are very picky about their knives—most choose one favorite knife and take it with them in their chef's kit wherever they go to cook. You can start the search for your cooking companion by trying out a few beginner-friendly knives found in the kitchen section in most stores. Look for one with a serrated edge, a sheath for storing it, and a medium size and weight.

THE BEST FIRST KNIFE

If you're just starting out using a knife, a nylon knife is perfect for slicing food and not your fingers.

THE PRO CHEF'S KNIFE

If you're used to knives already, upgrade to a stainless steel mini santoku knife with a serrated edge. This is like the Japanese santoku knives that professional chefs use but in a more easy-to-handle size.

MATERIALS
- **Beginner-friendly knife, such as a nylon or stainless steel serrated-edge knife**
- **Cutting board**

- **3 to 4 carrots**
- **3 to 4 large tomatoes**
- **3 to 4 cucumbers**

PART 1: MASTERING THE BASICS
From massive competition kitchens to miniature food truck counters, every kitchen has the same ground rules, and every professional chef follows them like second nature. Mastering these basic practices is the first step in this crash course.

WEAR CLOSED-TOE SHOES
Every restaurant kitchen and culinary school requires this because it protects you if something sharp or hot falls at your feet.

HOLD THE KNIFE AT THE BASE OF THE BLADE
For more control, do like the pros and grip the top of the base of the blade, closest to the handle, between your thumb and the side of your curled pointer finger, with the rest of your hand wrapped around the handle. With your hand in this position, you'll have a better grip than if you just held the handle alone. Practice holding the knife like this for a few minutes, until it feels comfortable.

CURL YOUR FINGERS UNDER
Take your knife-free hand and hold down the food you're going to cut. Before you slice anything, check how your fingers are positioned on the food. They should be curled down and inward toward your palm, not sticking straight out. If done properly, the knuckles right above your nails will stick out past the ends of your fingers. Cooks keep their fingers like this when cutting because if the knife touches your other hand, it will hit your knuckles instead of your fingertips. As you cut, you'll maintain this hand position. Practice holding a carrot like this and moving your fingers up and down the carrot until it feels natural.

KEEP THE TIP OF THE KNIFE ON THE CUTTING BOARD

Chefs chop so quickly because they never fully lift the knife—they just move the handle up and down and place the food closer to the handle, so that each movement is efficient and controlled. Spend a few minutes practicing this up-and-down movement on the cutting board, without any food to get in the way.

CHOPPING IS ABOUT CONSISTENCY

In culinary school, you're graded on the consistency of your cuts—can you get every piece to be the same size and shape?—not speed. Speed is nothing if your cuts are all over the place! As you practice your cuts below, start by moving as slowly as you can, pausing to inspect each piece and see if it's the same size as the one before. If you can get through a full vegetable with all the cuts being the same size and shape, then you can gradually pick up a bit of speed.

PART 2: THREE SUPER-USEFUL KNIFE CUTS TO PRACTICE

Once you feel comfortable using your knife just like the chefs do, you can start practicing your these super-handy, everyday-use knife cuts.

RONDELLE

You probably know how to do this cut already. A rondelle cut is basically just a slice of something round, like a coin. So anytime you slice a carrot, like for soup, for example, you're actually doing a rondelle cut. The trickiest part is getting all of your slices to be the same thickness.

1. Hold a carrot with your fingers curled under.

2. Slice a few times across the width, not the length, of the carrot, keeping the tip of the knife on the board and aiming for a ⅛-inch-thick slice.

3. Inspect your slices. Are they the same thickness? If not, slow down and focus on moving your knife just ⅛ of an inch up the carrot with each slice.

4. Keep practicing on more carrots until you've cut one whole carrot into consistent ⅛-inch slices.

MEDIUM DICE

The medium dice is one of the cuts you'll use the most in the kitchen. Anytime you read a recipe that calls for something "diced" without a size, this is a safe bet, since it's not too large and not too small. Ideally, a medium dice produces ½-inch cubes, but since most food isn't easily cut into such a perfect little cube, it's fine to cut pieces that are approximately ½ inch in size. This is a great cut to teach you how to adapt more rigid, perfectly measured cuts to the imperfect shape of common foods.

1. Slice a whole tomato in half, vertically.

2. Place the cut side of the tomato down on the board, then cut it into vertical slices that are about ½ inch thick. If you have a serrated or slightly dull knife, you may need to use a slight sawing motion to break the skin of the tomato.

3. Take each slice, lay it flat, and envision a ½ by ½-inch grid on it. Cut along those imaginary grid lines, so that each piece is about ½ inch on both sides. It won't be a perfect cube since the tomato has a round shape, and you may need to make more or fewer cuts depending on the size of your tomato. It's OK—this is more of a freestyle cut.

4. Inspect your dice—does the skin side of the tomato look pretty close to ½ by ½ inch? Keep practicing on the remaining slices until you've diced the whole tomato.

5. Practice on more tomatoes until you can achieve that ½-inch dice consistently. Increase your speed a little at a time while maintaining consistent sizes.

JULIENNE

The French word *julienne* means matchstick. Based off the name alone, you've probably already guessed what we're going for: a long, thin, matchstick shape. The julienne should be ⅛ inch thick, ⅛ inch deep, and about 2½ inches long. This cut lets you turn round vegetables, like cucumbers, into neat little rectangular shapes.

1. Cut the ends off a cucumber.

2. Holding the cucumber pointing away from you, and gripping one side of it tightly, cut a ⅛-inch piece off of the side, lengthwise. You'll now have one flat side of the cucumber.

3. Do the same on the opposite side.

4. You'll now have a cucumber with two flat sides. Place one of the flat sides down on the board, so it doesn't roll. Mentally (or literally!) measure about 2½-inch-long pieces of the cucumber, then cut the cucumber horizontally along those lines. You should now have two or three 2½-inch-long chunks of cucumber.

5. Take one of the pieces and hold it pointing away from you, flat side down. Make vertical cuts along it that are about ⅛ inch wide. You'll have wide, flat, almost strip-like pieces of cucumber.

6. Take one strip and lay it flat on the board, long side pointing away from you. Make another set of ⅛ inch vertical cuts along it. At this point, you've made your first set of matchsticks.

7. Continue with the remaining slices and then repeat steps 5 and 6 with the remaining chunks of cucumber.

8. Keep practicing on more cucumbers until you can get consistently sized matchsticks and can more easily visualize how to turn something round into cubed little matchsticks.

GRAB A GROWN-UP!

HOW TO MAKE YOUR OWN JERKY

Homemade jerky is one the of yummiest snacks to pack for your next adventure. It has a ton of protein, which makes you feel full and energized to climb that tree or play some kickball. When you make it yourself at home, you can dodge the processed ingredients that are in jerky from the store, and you can make it whatever flavor you want. (We love adding maple syrup for a jerky that tastes like maple bacon!) And did you know you can make jerky out of any meat: beef, chicken, pork, and even salmon? This recipe is super adaptable for any kind of meat and any quantity—just be sure you enlist an adult to help with the slicing and using the oven.

INGREDIENTS

- **2 pounds eye of round roast, sliced thin against the grain**
- **2 cloves garlic, minced**
- **¾ cup soy sauce**
- **¼ cup Worcestershire sauce**
- **¼ cup brown sugar**
- **2 teaspoons onion powder**
- **1 cup beef stock**

INSTRUCTIONS

1. In a large zip-top bag, combine all ingredients. Marinate in the refrigerator for 8 to 24 hours.

2. Ask an adult to preheat the oven to 170°F. Set out two cooling racks on two large baking sheets.

3. Remove the beef from the bag and pat dry on paper towels.

4. Evenly spread the meat on the cooling racks and cook for 2 to 3 hours with the oven door cracked open.

5. When the jerky is dry but still slightly pliable, remove from the oven and allow to cool.

6. Store in a zip-top bag for 2 to 3 weeks in the refrigerator.

TRAIL MIX, FIVE WAYS

We're calling this Trail Mix, Five Ways, but, really, with the goody grab bag below, you can make trail mix 850,668 ways. (Yes, we did the math!) That's because trail mix is just like life—it's going to be whatever you make of it, so it's best to make it out of exactly what you love. Scan through the lists below and think about what ingredients pop out at you . . . what sounds so yummy that you want it. Right. This. Second. Do all your favorites seem like they could go together? Or should you divvy up the spoils into two or three signature trail mixes? If you're packing up snacks for a bunch of people instead of crafting a personal mix just for you, jump right to the crowd-pleasing mixes section. Whatever trail you choose to get to your perfect mix, make sure to make plenty of it, since hands-on girls need lots of crunchy, salty, sweet fuel to tackle their adventures.

NUTTY
- **Almonds**
- **Peanuts**
- **Walnuts**
- **Cashews**
- **Macadamia nuts**
- **Pecans**
- **Pistachios**
- **Hazelnuts**

CRUNCHY
- **Sunflower seeds**
- **Flaxseeds**
- **Pumpkin seeds**
- **Wasabi peas**
- **Popcorn**
- **Granola**
- **Pretzels**
- **Animal crackers**

FRUITY
- **Raisins**
- **Banana chips**
- **Dried cranberries**
- **Dried cherries**
- **Dried apricots**
- **Dried apples**
- **Dried goji berries**
- **Freeze-dried blueberries**
- **Crystallized ginger**
- **Toasted coconut flakes**

SWEET

(Note: If you'll be on the trail with your mix on a hot day, go for candy-coated chocolate, like M&Ms, that won't melt as easily as chocolate chips, or maybe skip the chocolate altogether if it's going to be a scorcher.)

- **Milk chocolate chips**
- **Dark chocolate chunks**
- **White chocolate chunks**
- **Peanut butter chips**
- **M&Ms**
- **Reese's Pieces**
- **Chocolate-covered sunflower seeds**
- **Chocolate-covered raisins**
- **Cereal**
- **Gummy bears**
- **Sour gummies**
- **Runts**

A PINCH OF . . .

- **Sea salt**
- **Brown sugar**
- **Cayenne pepper**
- **Cinnamon**

My signature trail mix is _____.

CROWD-PLEASING TRAIL MIXES TO FUEL UP YOUR WHOLE SQUAD

Each recipe makes 4 to 5 cups of trail mix, perfect for sharing with 4 to 5 friends.

NUTTY–SALTY–CRUNCHY MIX

- **1½ cups cashews**
- **1½ cups pretzels**
- **1 cup pecans**
- **1 cup chocolate-covered sunflower seeds**
- **Pinch of sea salt**

FRUITY–CHEWY–CRISPY MIX

- **1 cup banana chips**
- **1 cup animal crackers**
- **1 cup dried cherries**
- **½ cup coconut flakes**
- **½ cup gummy bears**

SPICY SWEET–SOUR MIX

- **1 cup peanuts**
- **1 cup popcorn**
- **½ cup white chocolate**
- **½ cup crystallized ginger**
- **½ cup wasabi peas**
- **½ cup sour gummies**
- **Pinch of cayenne**

CHOCOLATE, CHOCOLATE, AND MORE CHOCOLATE MIX

- **1½ cups almonds**
- **1½ cups popcorn**
- **½ cup dark chocolate chunks**
- **½ cup chocolate-covered raisins**
- **½ cup chocolate-covered sunflower seeds**
- **Pinch of sea salt**

BERRIES ON BLAST MIX

- **1½ cups macadamia nuts**
- **¾ cup freeze-dried blueberries**
- **¾ cup dried cranberries**
- **½ cup dried cherries**
- **½ cup Runts**

INSTRUCTIONS

1. Combine ingredients in a large mixing bowl and stir until evenly mixed.

2. Divide into plastic baggies to take on the trail, or store in a glass jar or plastic container to keep at home.

DRYING FRUIT FOR ON-THE-GO

Just like jerky, fruit is really easy to dehydrate at home, and nothing is yummier and more flavorful than homemade. You can dry any fruit using this recipe—the trick is to make sure you use ripe fruit, slice it thinly, and bake it in the oven (with an adult's help) until it's dry and chewy, which will take more or less time depending on the fruit. The best part is that you can customize your dried fruit to be exactly how you like it. Try adding a sprinkle of cinnamon to apple slices or a dash of powdered peanut butter to banana slices and you'll have the most amazing dried fruit add-ins for your trail mix grab bag on page 185.

Makes 1 (11 x 17-inch) tray of dried fruit

INGREDIENTS
- **1 ripe apple or pear**
- **1 ripe banana**
- **½ cup ripe strawberries**

INSTRUCTIONS

1. Ask an adult to preheat the oven to 170°F.

2. Wash all the fruit, then prepare the strawberries and apples or pears by removing any stems, seeds, or cores. Then slice the fruits into ⅛-inch-thick sections. Peel the banana and slice into ⅛-inch-thick slices. Try to make all slices as uniform as possible so they'll dehydrate at the same rate. (If you want to practice your slicing skills, go to page 181!)

3. Arrange the slices on a nonstick or parchment paper–lined baking sheet, making sure none of the slices are touching each other or the edges of the sheet.

4. Bake for 3 to 5 hours (longer if your slices are thicker), checking on them every 30 minutes and flipping the slices every 1 hour. The fruit is ready when it's leathery and chewy but not too soft or too brittle.

5. Let the fruit sit in an open container overnight in the refrigerator to allow any lingering moisture to escape. Snack on it as is or give it a rough chop and toss it into your next trail mix. For leftovers, store in a sealed plastic or glass container at room temperature for 1 week or in the refrigerator for 2 to 3 weeks.

MEASURING AND WEIGHING LIKE A PRO

Cooking can seem complicated, but, really, it's just about following instructions. A recipe is nothing more than a list of supplies and directions, not much different from the volcano you built on page 16 or the checklist you run through each morning in your mind when you get ready for school. The main difference is that in cooking, we use more exact measurements, so refining your measuring skills is an important step on your path to becoming a top chef. Once you've had plenty of practice seeing what one tablespoon of minced garlic looks like, you can start eyeballing measurements like a pro. All that freestyling you see on TV cooking shows is built on a firm foundation of good measuring skills, so tuck these tips into your apron for the next time you're chopping your way through a recipe.

HOW TO MEASURE UNEVENLY SIZED DRY INGREDIENTS

For dry ingredients, you always want to use dry measuring cups, which are the cups with handles that stack into each other. Does your recipe call for 1 cup of chopped bell pepper? Chop your pepper into a medium dice (see page 182 to learn the medium dice), then pile it into the 1-cup measure. Some things, like peppers, are never going to fill a measuring cup perfectly and won't line up exactly with the top of a cup, but that's OK! With most savory recipes, it won't matter if you have a few scraps more or less of an ingredient. You'll also have empty nooks and crannies in the cup, but as long as the pepper or any other oddly shaped ingredient is mostly level with the top of the cup, you're good to go.

HOW TO MEASURE EVENLY SIZED DRY INGREDIENTS

If your recipe calls for something dry and evenly sized, like a cup of uncooked rice, you can use your dry measure cup to scoop the ingredients right out of the bag or jar. Since individual grains of rice or sugar are uniform in size, your cup will be entirely full, and you will need to level off the top to get rid of the extra. The best way to level a cup is to take a regular old butter knife and scrape the flat edge of the knife across the top of the measuring cup. You could really use anything that has a flat edge to it, as long as it scrapes evenly across the top of your cup. Use this technique for all granular or fine ingredients, like rice, sugar, and salt, as long as it's not a baking recipe (see more on that below). It may seem nitpicky to level off the measure, but for some ingredients and recipes, even a little bit too much of an ingredient at this stage can make a difference in the finished dish. For example, ¼ cup of uncooked rice will balloon into ¾ cup of cooked rice. And the same thing goes for even smaller measurements, like a tablespoon. One mounded tablespoon of salt might be way too salty in a recipe, but a leveled-off tablespoon would be perfection.

HOW TO MEASURE LIQUIDS

For liquids, you'll need another measuring tool: the liquid measuring cup, which is usually plastic or glass and has measurements marked along the side. This tool will measure fluid ounces instead of ounces by weight, so 1 cup will equal 8 fluid ounces. You'll want to use a liquid measuring cup with any ingredient that levels itself, so even thicker ingredients, like raw eggs, batter, or yogurt, would be best measured in this. With a liquid measure, you're watching for a phenomenon called the meniscus. The meniscus is the natural curve in a liquid when it's in a container—because the of the unique composition of water and other liquid molecules, they tend to "stick" to the edges of a container. If you get down to eye level with your liquid measure, you might notice that the liquid at the edges is ever so slightly higher than the liquid in the center. That curve is the meniscus, and the accurate measurement is at the lowest part of the curve, toward the curve's center. In most recipes you won't need to be this precise, but getting eye level with your measuring cup is a great habit to pick up for when you embark on a baking project.

HOW TO MEASURE AND WEIGH INGREDIENTS FOR BAKING

When it comes to savory cooking, you can usually aim for close-but-not-perfect with your measurements, and your food will come out delicious even if you have a few extra peppers or a little bit of extra rice in your finished dish. But with baking, precision is key. That's because baking is all about the ratios of wet ingredients to dry ingredients, so having a few splashes too much of milk or an extra tablespoon of flour can make your cupcakes too wet or too dry. If you want to stick to your dry measuring cups for baking, then the big thing to remember is to spoon the flour into your cup, not scoop it out of the bag like you can do with rice. Take a regular spoon and scoop flour from the bag into your cup until it's overfull, then level off the top so it's flat. Don't smash or press the flour into the cup, since that will actually compress the tiny little grains and give you more flour than you really want.

Or, if you want to up your game, do like the pastry chefs do and weigh your baking ingredients. Many baking recipes will give you two measurements: the dry measure, which would read "1 cup all-purpose flour," and the weight measure, which would read "4¼ ounces," or "120 grams," which is the metric equivalent (see page 194 to learn more about the metric system). You'll get the most accurate measurement by weight, and most digital kitchen scales are cheap, easy to use, and small enough to tuck into a drawer. To measure by weight, first put your measuring cup on the scale, then zero it out, since we don't care about the weight of the cup itself. Then follow the instructions above to spoon flour into the cup until the scale reads 120 grams, or whatever weight you're aiming for. Now you have the perfect quantity of flour you need. If you're feeling scientific, experiment by weighing all different kinds of ingredients—you'll be surprised to discover that 1 cup of whole wheat flour or 1 cup of almond flour aren't the same weight as all-purpose flour!

WHAT IS THE METRIC SYSTEM, AND WHY DON'T WE USE IT?

If you grew up with the American measuring system, then you've probably encountered the "meter," "liter," and "gram" only a few times and wondered why on earth there are so many ways of measuring things. After all, wouldn't it be easier if we all used the same system and stuck to measuring things in feet, inches, pounds, and ounces? Well, believe it or not, the U.S. is one of the few places on the planet that still uses those measurements, which are called the imperial or customary system. Everyone else is on the metric system! The metric system is also called the International System of Units, or SI System, and it was developed to simplify and standardize measurements across the world.

Long before the metric system, most countries measured things according to body parts—so a foot was meant to be about the size of a human foot. But anyone can see the problem in that: your foot is probably nowhere near the size of your parent's foot, right? And can you imagine what might happen if a recipe called for a handful of salt or a thumb-length of butter? One person would end up with a way over-salted and greasy dish, and the next person would be eating a bland, dry meal. Believe it or not, people actually measured things this way. Before the SI system was developed, different towns all used different systems, and the measurement world was like the lawless Wild West, where almost anything was acceptable.

This ridiculousness continued until the French Revolution of 1789. During this revolution, the new French government had their heart set on bringing back order and fairness to France, and this goal included dealing with their nation's chaotic measurement practices. Government leaders brought together a group of leading French scientists who finally said *"Non!"* to inconsistency and unstandardized measurements. Using their combined brainpower, these scientists studied theories formulated by previous mathematicians to create a logical measuring system based on units of ten. Their method of measuring became a success in France and garnered many fans, including one very powerful leader, Napoléon Bonaparte.

Recognizable by his first name alone, Napoléon rose to power during the French Revolution and even crowned himself the first emperor of France. But as a power-hungry politician, reigning over the whole of France wasn't good enough for him. Napoléon planned to raise an empire that stretched his authority across Europe and, eventually, the world! For over a decade, he conquered more and more territory, with no end in sight. Whenever he took over an area, he declared that the inhabitants were now citizens of the French empire and must follow French customs and practices, including using the French metric system.

Now, from our perspective in time, we know that the French empire did not last forever (just look at a modern map of Europe if you want to double-check), yet the metric system survived. Even after the empire fell, many newly formed countries experimented with different measuring systems, but all decided that the metric system worked the best. As more countries adopted the metric system, it became a universal language of measurement that made international interactions, like trade, much easier and fairer for everyone.

But if the rest of the world eventually got on board with the metric system, why didn't the U.S. jump on the bandwagon? Well, like many things in the U.S., it came down to a separation of powers between the federal and state governments. In 1988, the federal government decided to switch over to metric measurements for all of its work, but this decision did not affect the states. It's now up to each state to decide whether to make the change and, because opinions vary so widely among states, there's no consensus. Instead, the U.S. now has a patchwork of the two measurement systems that differs between levels of government, states, industries, and so on. So, will the U.S. ever make a final decision? In the end, any unification effort will probably have to be orchestrated by the federal government, but with so many proponents for the states to choose for themselves, this would be a tricky move. What do you think? Would you rather stick to our current measuring system or adopt the metric system?

TWO DINNERS (AND A DESSERT!) YOU CAN MAKE IN A JIFFY

Every chef has a signature dish—that one thing they make that everyone goes crazy for. And it's fun to have one or two recipes in your back pocket that you can practice making over and over again until you barely need to look at the recipe to whip it up. So what should your signature dish be? Start by thinking about your #1 favorite food. What one thing do you *love* to eat and wish you could have all the time? Begin there, because hey, even if you mess up the first few times you make it, at least it'll still be pizza, pasta, pie, or whatever it is you like.

If you want to add two super-simple dinners and a dessert to your arsenal of recipes, try out these tried-and-true favorites the next time you and your grown-up are in the kitchen together. These recipes are crowd-pleasers, really easy to make, and so yummy that you'll want to keep making them over and over. You'll also be able to put the sautéing you learned about on page 177 into practice here. And remember: chefs like you love to let their creativity flow, so don't be afraid to experiment with substitutions and make these recipes your own!

ONE-POT BROCCOLI–CHEDDAR PASTA

Yes, you can make a pasta dish in just one pot! This is such an easy, simple, comforting dish to master, and all it takes are seven basic ingredients to whip up this creamy, cheesy wonder.

Serves 4

INGREDIENTS

- **Salt and pepper**
- **8 cups broccoli florets, fresh or frozen**
- **1 pound short pasta (like shells, penne, or rigatoni)**
- **4 tablespoons olive oil**
- **5 cloves garlic, minced**
- **¼ cup parmesan**
- **¼ cup cheddar**
- **½ cup plain Greek yogurt**

INSTRUCTIONS

1. Fill a large pot with water and place it over high heat. Add 1 tablespoon of salt. While you wait for your water to boil, chop the broccoli into small florets, about 1 inch.

2. Once the water is boiling, add the pasta and broccoli at the same time. Stir well to keep the pasta from sticking to itself or the bottom of the pot. Check the recommended cooking time on the box of pasta, and set a timer for the lower end of the range, so your pasta will be al dente.

3. When the timer goes off, carefully scoop 1 cup of water out of the pot, then ask an adult to drain the pasta and broccoli for you. Leave the pasta and broccoli in the drainer for now.

4. Place the pot back over medium heat, then add 2 tablespoons of the olive oil and then, 30 seconds later, the garlic. Sauté until the garlic is golden but not dark brown, 1 to 2 minutes. Add the pasta and broccoli to the pot and mix well.

5. Reduce the heat to low and add the parmesan, cheddar, yogurt, and remaining olive oil. Stir well, so your cheeses melt. Mash up any big chunks of broccoli, and add a few splashes of the reserved pasta water to keep the sauce loose and moist. Taste the pasta—see if you think it needs more salt; if you want the cheese sauce to be looser, add a few more splashes of pasta water. Keep adjusting until you like the taste and texture. Add a few grinds of black pepper, if you like that.

6. Serve warm and dig into the comforting goodness you made for yourself!

DOES THE PASTA SHAPE MATTER?

Most short pasta shapes are pretty interchangeable, and so are most long pasta shapes. So if a recipe calls for spaghetti, you can totally use fettucine, linguine, or angel hair, and if it calls for a short pasta shape like rigatoni, shells, elbows, and penne are usually just as good.

WHAT IS "AL DENTE" ANYWAY?

Al dente is an Italian phrase that means "to the tooth," and it's what people call pasta that still has a little bit of bite to it and isn't too soft or mushy. Pasta that's perfectly al dente is much yummier and enjoyable to eat than overcooked pasta, so always aim to undercook your pasta by 1 to 2 minutes, since it'll keep cooking even after you've drained it.

WHY RESERVE THE PASTA WATER?

Did you know that pasta water is magic? When pasta boils in water, it releases a lot of its starch, so the remaining water is a starchy, salty mix that's perfect for bringing together a pasta sauce. The starch helps your sauce thicken while the salt will help season it, so it's always a good idea to set aside a cup of water before you drain your pasta. Italian chefs swear by this trick, and even though they might not use the whole cup of reserved water, they know that even a few splashes can make all the difference for bringing a dish together.

MAKE YOUR OWN TACO BAR, HOSTED BY YOU

Taco Tuesday, Taco Wednesday, Taco Thursday . . . we could eat tacos every night. And the best part about tacos is that you can make them differently each and every time—there really are 1,001 ways to fill a taco! But the classic ground beef taco is a classic for a reason. It's packed with flavor, easy to make, and just as delicious with one topping as it is with every topping under the taco sun. And if you learn to make your own taco seasoning, your taco meat will come out so much more flavorful and delicious than using the regular old seasoning packet that comes with a store-bought taco kit. Once you master this basic taco filling and homemade seasoning, you can lay out the taco spread of your dreams any night.

Serves 4

DIY TACO SEASONING
- **1 tablespoon chili powder**
- **2 teaspoons ground cumin**
- **1 teaspoon dried oregano**
- **1 teaspoon garlic powder**
- **¼ teaspoon paprika**
- **1 teaspoon salt**
- **1 teaspoon black pepper**

INGREDIENTS
- **1 tablespoon olive oil**
- **1 pound ground beef**

TOPPINGS MENU (CHOOSE AND CHOP WHATEVER TOPPINGS YOU WANT TO OFFER AT YOUR BAR!)
- **Lettuce, thinly sliced**
- **Tomatoes, medium dice**
- **Avocado, medium dice**
- **Limes, cut into quarters**
- **Scallions, sliced**
- **White onion, small dice**
- **Cilantro leaves**
- **Sliced black olives**
- **Sour cream**
- **Shredded cheddar**
- **Taco shells**
- **Flour or corn tortillas**
- **Salsa**
- **Hot sauce**

INSTRUCTIONS

1. Combine all the spices for the taco seasoning in a small bowl; set aside. Choose your toppings from the toppings menu above, chop anything that needs to be chopped, and put everything in its own little bowl on the table.

2. In a large skillet over medium-high heat, add the olive oil. Swirl the skillet around until the oil coats the bottom of the pan. Add the ground beef and break it up with your spoon until it's a crumble instead of big chunks.

3. Once your meat is browned and no pieces are pink anymore (6 to 8 minutes), ask an adult to pick up the skillet and drain out the liquid fat.

4. With the skillet back over medium-high heat, add the taco seasoning and ½ cup water. Mix the seasoning in well, and when the water has mostly evaporated but the meat is still moist, you're done! Serve your taco meat right in the skillet to keep it warm at the table.

THREE-INGREDIENT PEANUT BUTTER COOKIES

These cookies are so ridiculously easy you can make them in less than five minutes of hands-on time. That means that as long as you have some peanut butter, sugar, and eggs in the house, you could be just a few minutes away from warm, gooey, peanut butter-y cookies.

Makes 12 cookies

INGREDIENTS

- **1 cup peanut butter**
- **1 cup sugar**
- **1 egg**

INSTRUCTIONS

1. Ask an adult to preheat the oven to 350°F. Line a baking sheet with parchment paper or foil.

2. In a medium bowl, mix the peanut butter, sugar, and egg together with a large spoon until smooth and evenly incorporated into a cookie batter.

3. Using a tablespoon measure, measure out 2 tablespoons of batter per cookie, then roll each lump between both hands until it forms a ball.

4. Space the balls in four rows of three cookies each on your baking sheet with each cookie being at least 3 inches apart. With a fork, press down on each cookie ball in one direction and then in the other direction, so you get a crosshatch of ridges on top of your cookie.

5. Bake for 15 to 20 minutes until firm but still slightly chewy. Let cool for 1 to 2 minutes before gobbling them up.

Badges for Hands-On Girls

Badges are the way hands-on girls mark and celebrate their accomplishments, and you can earn one any time you check off the criteria for a particular badge. Wearing a badge is a statement to the world that you're brave, you're not afraid to try new things, and you're proud of yourself, no matter what you take on.

THE SCIENTIST BADGE is awarded to a hands-on girl who has completed five activities from Chapter 1.

THE TRAILBLAZER BADGE is awarded to a hands-on girl who has completed five activities from Chapter 2.

THE ATHLETE BADGE
is awarded to a hands-on
girl who has completed five
activities from Chapter 3.

THE ARTIST BADGE
is awarded to a hands-on
girl who has completed five
activities from Chapter 4.

THE BUILDER BADGE
is awarded to a hands-on
girl who has completed five
activities from Chapter 5.

THE CHEF BADGE
is awarded to a hands-on
girl who has completed five
activities from Chapter 6.

THE JANE-OF-ALL-TRADES BADGE
is awarded to a hands-on
girl who has completed one
activity from each chapter.

THE OUTDOORSY BADGE

is awarded to a hands-on girl who has completed six outdoor activities from any chapter.

THE INDOORSY BADGE

is awarded to a hands-on girl who has completed six indoor activities from any chapter.

THE GOOD FRIEND BADGE

is awarded to a hands-on girl who has performed an act of kindness for a friend.

THE GOOD NEIGHBOR BADGE

is awarded to a hands-on girl who has performed an act of kindness for a neighbor.

THE GOOD CITIZEN BADGE

is awarded to a hands-on girl who has performed an act of kindness for the planet.

FURTHER READING

LET'S BE SCIENTISTS!

101 Great Science Experiments: A Step-by-Step Guide
Neil Ardley

The Everything Kids' Science Experiments Book: Boil Ice, Float Water, Measure Gravity— Challenge the World Around You!
Tom Robinson

Kitchen Science Lab for Kids: 52 Family-Friendly Experiments from Around the House
Liz Lee Heinecke

Awesome Physics Experiments for Kids: 40 Fun Science Projects and Why They Work
Erica L. Colón, Ph.D.

Real Chemistry Experiments: 40 Exciting STEAM Activities for Kids
Edward P. Zovinka, Ph.D.

LET'S BE TRAILBLAZERS!

Exploring Nature Activity Book for Kids: 50 Creative Projects to Spark Curiosity in the Outdoors
Kim Andrews

Exploring Nature Journal for Kids: Observe and Record the Outdoors
Kim Andrews

Ultimate Bugopedia: The Most Complete Bug Reference Ever
Darlyne Murawski, Nancy Honovich

The 175 Best Camp Games: A Handbook for Leaders
Kathleen Fraser, Laura Fraser, and Mary Fraser

Survivor Kid: A Practical Guide to Wilderness Survival
Denise Long

LET'S BE ATHLETES!

Women in Sports: 50 Fearless Athletes Who Played to Win
Rachel Ignotofsky

303 Tween-Approved Exercises and Active Games
Kimberly Wechsler

101 Things to Do Outside: Loads of Fantastically Fun Reasons to Get Up, Get Out, and Get Active!
Creative Team of Weldon Owen

The Essential Karate Book: For White Belts, Black Belts and All Levels In Between
Graeme Lund

The Ultimate Book of Family Card Games
Oliver Ho

LET'S BE ARTISTS!
Adventure Girls!: Crafts and Activities for Curious, Creative, Courageous Girls
Nicole Duggan

Rip All the Pages!: 52 Tear-Out Adventures for Creative Writers
Karen Benke

Art Lab for Kids: 52 Creative Adventures in Drawing, Painting, Printmaking, Paper, and Mixed Media-For Budding Artists of All Ages
Susan Schwake

Modern Calligraphy for Kids: A Step-by-Step Guide and Workbook for Lettering Fun
Sally Sanders

Notebook Doodles Go Girl!
Jess Volinski

LET'S BE BUILDERS!
Sticks and Stones: A Kid's Guide to Building and Exploring in the Great Outdoors
Melissa Lennig

Wood Shop: Handy Skills and Creative Building Projects for Kids
Margaret Larson

Easy Wood Carving for Children: Fun Whittling Projects for Adventurous Kids
Frank Egholm

The Kids' Building Workshop: 15 Woodworking Projects for Kids and Parents to Build Together
Craig Robertson, Barbara Robertson

Awesome Engineering Activities for Kids: 50+ Exciting STEAM Projects to Design and Build
Christina Schul

LET'S BE CHEFS!

The Complete Cookbook for Young Chefs
America's Test Kitchen Kids

Cooking Class Global Feast!: 44 Recipes That Celebrate the World's Cultures
Deanna F. Cook

Awesome Kitchen Science Experiments for Kids: 50 STEAM Projects You Can Eat!
Megan Olivia Hall

20 Recipes Kids Should Know
Esme Washburn

The Ultimate Kids' Baking Book: 60 Easy & Fun Dessert Recipes for Every Holiday, Birthday, Milestone and More
Tiffany Dahle

INDEX

ACKNOWLEDGMENTS

Thank you to hands-on girls everywhere, who bring all the adventure and fun to our days. A huge thank-you to Carson Watlington, for your editorial flair and passion for this project. Thanks to Alexis Seabrook, for the sweet and sassy illustrations that gave this book its sparkle.

Thank you to Allison Adler, who believed in this project and its mission from the start and has been so hands-on in championing it, as well as to the entire team at Andrews McMeel—Elizabeth Garcia, Diane Marsh, and Chuck Harper for turning an idea into a beautiful and cheery book.

Thank you to Maria Ribas for sparking this idea and bringing it to life, Ellen Scordato for her expert guidance, and the entire Stonesong team for creating a place where hands-on girls can tackle anything.

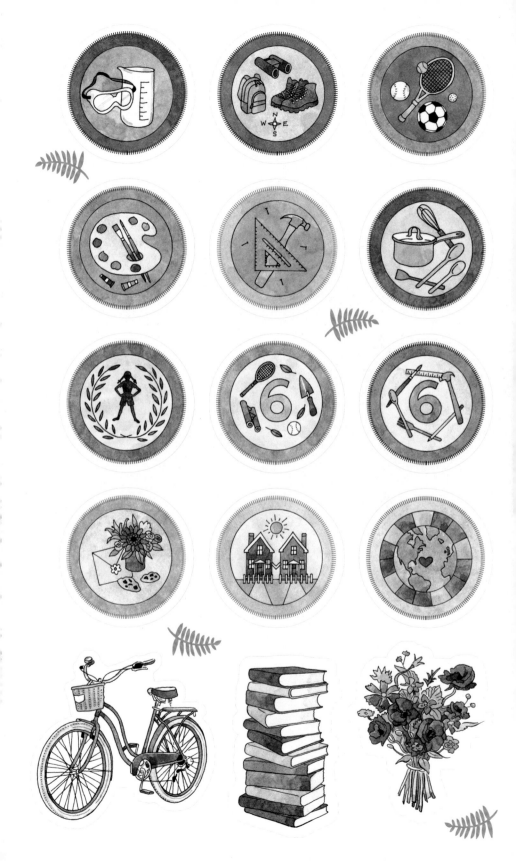